CUSTOM CURRICULUM

This is the property of
Children's Ministries Department
Trans European Division of SDA Church
119 St Peter's Street
St Albans AL1 3EY
England

D1809766

Your Bible's Alive!

Fran and Jill
Sciacca

Stan
Campbell

David C. Cook Publishing Co.
Elgin, Illinois—Weston, Ontario

Custom Curriculum
Your Bible's Alive!

© 1994 David C. Cook Publishing Co.

All rights reserved. Except for the reproducible student sheets, which may be copied for ministry use, no part of this book may be reproduced in any form without the written permission of the publisher, unless otherwise noted in the text.

Unless otherwise noted, Scripture quotations are from the Holy Bible, New International Version (NIV), © 1973, 1978, 1984 by International Bible Society. Used by permission of Zondervan Bible Publishers.

Published by David C. Cook Publishing Co.
850 North Grove Ave., Elgin, IL 60120
Cable address: DCCOOK
Series creator: John Duckworth
Series editor: Randy Southern
Editor: Randy Southern
Option writers: Stan Campbell, Nelson E. Copeland, Jr., and Sue Reck
Designer: Bill Paetzold
Cover illustrator: David Goldin
Inside illustrator: Eric Masi
Printed in U.S.A.

ISBN: 0-7814-5152-3

CONTENTS

About the Authors

Stan Campbell has been a youth worker for over nineteen years and has written several books on youth ministry including the BibleLog series (SonPower) and the Quick Studies series (David C. Cook). He and his wife, Pam, are youth directors at Lisle Bible Church in Lisle, Illinois.

Nelson E. Copeland, Jr., is a nationally known speaker and the author of several youth resources including *Great Games for City Kids* (Youth Specialties) and *A New Agenda for Urban Youth* (Winston-Derek). He is president of the Christian Education Coalition for African-American Leadership (CECAAL), an organization dedicated to reinforcing educational and cultural excellence among urban teenagers. He also serves as youth pastor at the First Baptist Church in Morton, Pennsylvania.

Sue Reck is an editor for Chariot Family Products. She is also a free-lance curriculum writer. She has worked with young people in Sunday school classes, youth groups, and camp settings.

You've Made the Right Choice!

Thanks for choosing **Custom Curriculum!** We think your choice says at least three things about you:

(1) You know your group pretty well, and want your program to fit that group like a glove;

(2) You like having options instead of being boxed in by some far-off curriculum editor;

(3) You have a small mole on your left forearm, exactly two inches below the elbow.

OK, so we were wrong about the mole. But if you like having choices that help you tailor meetings to fit your kids, **Custom Curriculum** *is* the best place to be.

Going through Customs

In this (and every) **Custom Curriculum** volume, you'll find

• five great sessions you can use anytime, in any order.

• reproducible student handouts, at least one per session.

• a truckload of options for adapting the sessions to your group (more about that in a minute).

• a helpful get-you-ready article by a youth expert.

• clip art for making posters, fliers, and other kinds of publicity to get kids to your meetings.

Each **Custom Curriculum** session has three to six steps. No matter how many steps a session has, it's designed to achieve these goals:

• *Getting together.* Using an icebreaker activity, you'll help kids be glad they came to the meeting.

• *Getting thirsty.* Why should kids care about your topic? Why should they care what the Bible has to say about it? You'll want to take a few minutes to earn their interest before you start pouring the "living water."

• *Getting the Word.* By exploring and discussing carefully selected passages, you'll find out what God has to say.

• *Getting the point.* Here's where you'll help kids make the leap from principles to nitty-gritty situations they are likely to face.

• *Getting personal.* What should each group member do as a result of this session? You'll help each person find a specific "next step" response that works for him or her.

Each session is written to last 45 to 60 minutes. But what if you have less time—or more? No problem! **Custom Curriculum** is all about . . . options!

What Are My Options?

Every **Custom Curriculum** session gives you fourteen kinds of options:

• *Extra Action*—for groups that learn better when they're physically moving (instead of just reading, writing, and discussing).

• *Combined Junior High/High School*—to use when you're mixing age levels, and an activity or case study would be too "young" or "old" for part of the group.

• *Small Group*—for adapting activities that would be tough with groups of fewer than eight kids.

• *Large Group*—to alter steps for groups of more than twenty kids.

• *Urban*—for fitting sessions to urban facilities and multiethnic (especially African-American) concerns.

• *Heard It All Before*—for fresh approaches that get past the defenses of kids who are jaded by years in church.

• *Little Bible Background*—to use when most of your kids are strangers to the Bible, or haven't made a Christian commitment.

• *Mostly Guys*—to focus on guys' interests and to substitute activities they might be more enthused about.

• *Mostly Girls*—to address girls' concerns and to substitute activities they might prefer.

• *Extra Fun*—for longer, more "rowdy" youth meetings where the emphasis is on fun.

• *Short Meeting Time*—tips for condensing the session to 30 minutes or so.

• *Fellowship & Worship*—for building deeper relationships or enabling kids to praise God together.

• *Media*—to spice up meetings with video, music, or other popular media.

• *Sixth Grade*—appearing only in junior high/middle school volumes, this option helps you change steps that sixth graders might find hard to understand or relate to.

• *Extra Challenge*—appearing only in high school volumes, this option lets you crank up the voltage for kids who are ready for more Scripture or more demanding personal application.

Each kind of option is offered twice in each session. So in this book, you get *almost 150* ways to tweak the meetings to fit your group!

Customizing a Session

All right, you may be thinking. *With all of these options flying around, how do I put a session together? I don't have a lot of time, you know.*

We know! That's why we've made **Custom Curriculum** as easy to follow as possible. Let's take a look at how you might prepare an actual meeting. You can do that in four easy steps:

(1) *Read the basic session plan.* Start by choosing one or more of the goals listed at the beginning of the session. You have three to pick from: a goal that emphasizes *knowledge,* one that stresses *understanding,* and one that emphasizes *action.* Choose one or more, depending on what *you* want to accomplish. Then read the basic plan to see what will work for you and what might not.

(2) *Choose your options.* You don't *have* to use any options at all; the basic session plan would work well for many groups, and you may want

to stick with it if you have absolutely no time to consider options. But if you want a more perfect fit, check out your choices.

As you read the basic session plan, you'll see small symbols in the margin. Each symbol stands for a different kind of option. When you see a symbol, it means that kind of option is offered for that step. Turn to the options section (which can be found immediately following the Repro Resources for each session), look for the category indicated by the symbol, and you'll see that option explained.

Let's say you have a small group, mostly guys who get bored if they don't keep moving. You'll want to keep an eye out for three kinds of options: Small Group, Mostly Guys, and Extra Action. As you read the basic session, you might spot symbols that tell you there are Small Group options for Step 1 and Step 3—maybe a different way to play a game so that you don't need big teams, and a way to cover several Bible passages when just a few kids are looking them up. Then you see symbols telling you that there are Mostly Guys options for Step 2 and Step 4—perhaps a substitute activity that doesn't require too much self-disclosure, and a case study guys will relate to. Finally you see symbols indicating Extra Action options for Step 2 and Step 3—maybe an active way to get kids' opinions instead of handing out a survey, and a way to act out some verses instead of just looking them up.

After reading the options, you might decide to use four of them. You base your choices on your personal tastes and the traits of your group that you think are most important right now. **Custom Curriculum** offers you more options than you'll need, so you can pick your current favorites and plug others into future meetings if you like.

(3) *Use the checklist.* Once you've picked your options, keep track of them with the simple checklist that appears at the end of each option section (just before the start of the next session plan). This little form gives you a place to write down the materials you'll need too—since they depend on the options you've chosen.

(4) *Get your stuff together.* Gather your materials; photocopy any Repro Resources (reproducible student sheets) you've decided to use. And . . . you're ready!

The Custom Curriculum Challenge

Your kids are fortunate to have you as their leader. You see them not as a bunch of generic teenagers, but as real, live, unique kids. You care whether you really connect with them. That's why you're willing to take a few extra minutes to tailor your meetings to fit.

It's a challenge to work with real, live kids, isn't it? We think you deserve a standing ovation for taking that challenge. And we pray that **Custom Curriculum** helps you shape sessions that shape lives for Jesus Christ and His kingdom.

—The Editors

How to Handle a Double-Edged Sword

by Fran and Jill Sciacca

As you introduce *Your Bible's Alive!* keep in mind that your group probably consists of a mixed bag of Bible students. At one extreme, you may have kids who don't know Chronicles from Corinthians. At the other extreme, you may have some whose eyes have glazed over from too much Bible input and too little output. As a high school Bible teacher, I'm faced with both types each day. You may safely assume one thing about almost *all* of your kids: They probably have an incomplete understanding of what the Bible is.

Someone wisely said, "The Bible is a window into the very heart and mind of God Himself. Don't spend your life merely polishing the glass!" I like this statement because it is consistent with the Bible's own description of itself. In speaking of Jesus, the Living Word, John wrote, "No one has ever seen God, but God the One and Only, who is at the Father's side, has made him known" (John 1:18). God became a human in order to save human beings. But there remains the staggering reality that deep within the purposes of God, the intention was also present that humans could know more fully what the Lord is like. The Incarnation was intended to reveal the very nature and character of God to us. Therefore, the Bible *really* is a "window" into the heart and mind of God. With it, we can explore His thoughts and purpose for our life on this perplexing planet. Help your group members see the incredible truth that what they hold in their hands is not a mere book; it is a window through which we can see and know God.

There Are People on These Pages, Not Just Print!

The Bible is a real book about real people. God has painstakingly filled the pages of His Word with accounts of men, women, children, kings, queens, heroes, and failures. In glowing technicolor we see the results of good choices, and the consequences of bad choices. Paul's statement in Romans 15:4 ("For everything that was written in the past was written to teach us, so that through endurance and the encouragement of the Scriptures we might have hope") highlights one of God's intentions for spending so much time on *people* in the Bible. He wants us to *learn* from them!

High school students relate best to real-life people. In *Your Bible's Alive!* you will have avenues of opportunity to let biblical principles take on human form as you help group members see that the Bible is a book about people *like them.* Doors will open for discussions about deep (possibly painful) truths, and *you* will not be doing the "talking." Your Bible character can do most of the teaching for you!

Don't be afraid to discuss the failures you find in the Bible. Many of today's teens have a personal resumé filled with incidents they would like to forget. Likewise, the Bible contains stories of men and women who have failed. But some repented, and found forgiveness and hope. They learned from their mistakes and moved on with their lives. Other's didn't. Too often, we parade a string of successes before our teens, assuming that they will be challenged to higher living. What really needs to happen, however, is for kids to recognize that the Bible addresses ordinary struggling people just like them.

Looking through the Writer's Eyes

I'll never forget one class period when I was trying to teach the importance of properly interpreting Scripture. I took a note that a student had written to me and slowly read it to the class. After each paragraph, I would make some sort of interpretation of what the letter meant to me. I deliberately distorted the obvious meaning. When I finished, my students were frustrated. It was unfair, they said, for me to put my own interpretation into the words of the note. They all insisted that the student who wrote the note meant specific things by the words he or she had chosen. I had no business, they said, putting my own personal interpretation into the person's words. My obligation was to understand what the writer meant, not what I perceived he or she meant.

The same principle holds true regarding God's Word. Help your group members see that we need to place ourselves in the role of the first readers of any Bible book. Teach your kids to ask questions like "What was going on when this letter was written?" and "Why was this letter written?" Just as I had no right to reinterpret my student's note, we cannot preface a statement from God's Word with "Well, *to me* this passage means . . ." or "What *I* think this means is . . ." The author used the words he did for a reason.

You may also want to bring in a Bible encyclopedia, dictionary, and/or commentary. Introduce your group members to enlightening and helpful works that have been written to help us better understand God's Word. Often, what seems confusing or even contradictory when we read or study God's Word is simply a matter of understanding the culture or context of the passage.

Balancing Relevance and Reverence

Because of the variety and creativity in humanity, the Bible is full of unusual, sometimes even comical stories. You can have some good-natured fun with these stories, but be careful in the process. Some youth workers assume that the Bible is not relevant for today's teen; so they seek to *make it relevant.* In the process, the Bible is sometimes cheapened. Remember, God's truth is *always* relevant because its message is eternal. The problem is not relevancy, it is comprehension. When young people understand a passage of Scripture, it becomes personal and applicable to their lives. Do not sacrifice a sense of *reverence* for the Bible in an attempt to prove "relevance."

Prophecy's Primary Purpose

Teens turn to prophecy full of curiosity and intrigue. Every year, my students grown in disbelief when they discover that we're only going to spend one day on the Book of Revelation. (I teach a year-long Bible survey class.) Young people are attracted to topics that tend to generate a lot of heat, but very little light!

God has given us a clear statement on the purpose of predictive prophecy in II Peter 3:11, 12, 14: "Since everything will be destroyed in this way, what kind of people ought you to be? You ought to live holy and godly lives as you look forward to the day of God and speed its coming. . . . So then, dear friends, since you are looking forward to this, make every effort to be found spotless, blameless and at peace with him."

We have a sneak preview (but not the whole picture) of the last page of history. We know that this life is a gateway into eternity. We know that God will be glorified and Satan will be crushed. But we are not to focus on finding out *when* these things will happen. Help your group members understand that our knowledge of the Lord's return should cause us to live our daily lives in such a way that we are found "blameless" when He appears.

Your Bible's Alive! is designed to help your group members discover and embrace the truth of Hebrews 4:12: "For the word of God is living and active. Sharper than any double-edged sword, it penetrates even to dividing soul and spirit, joints and marrow; it judges the thoughts and attitudes of the heart."

In the process of preparing for this course, I trust that you will be stimulated yourself to become a faithful student of Scripture. I teach the Bible as a career. But I know that my most important message must be to communicate a love for God's Word rather than just a knowledge of what He has said in it. Trust me, the best teaching tool to use with this creative curriculum is your own life. If your group members see that the Word of God is changing your life and leading you to a more intimate walk with God, *they* will be challenged to see the Scripture come alive for themselves. What a *privilege!*

Fran and Jill Sciacca have been involved in youth ministry for nearly two decades. Fran is a graduate of Denver Seminary. He has been teaching Christian high school Bible since 1980. Jill has a degree in journalism and sociology and is a full-time homemaker and free-lance writer/editor. She has written for Discipleship Journal *and* Decision *magazine, and has served on the editorial team for the* Youth Bible *(Word, Inc.). Fran and Jill coauthored* Lifelines *(Zondervan), an award-winning Bible study series for high schoolers. Fran is the author of the best-selling Bible study,* To Walk and Not Grow Weary *(NavPress), as well as* Generation at Risk *(Moody), and* Wounded Saints *(Baker). Fran and Jill have four children—two daughters and two sons. The Sciaccas live in Alabaster, Alabama.*

Publicity Clip Art

The images on these two pages are designed to help you promote this course within your church and community. Feel free to photocopy anything here and adapt it to fit your publicity needs. The stuff on this page could be used as a flier that you send or hand out to kids—or as a bulletin insert. The stuff on the next page could be used to add visual interest to newsletters, calendars, bulletin boards, or other promotions. Be creative and have fun!

Watch Bible Characters Come to Life Before Your Very Eyes!

If you think Jonah was just a guy who took a weird fishing trip and David was just a guy who had good aim with a slingshot, you're in for a big surprise. Join us as we begin a new course called *Your Bible's Alive!* You'll discover some incredible facts about these and other Bible characters. Facts that you may never have heard before. Facts that may leave you eager to learn more.

Who:

When:

Where:

Questions? Call:

Your Bible's Alive!

Your Bible's Alive!

Find out what the Bible has to say.

"We're just looking for the truth."

SESSION

1 By the Book

YOUR GOALS FOR THIS SESSION:

Choose one or more

- [ ] To help kids see that the Bible, as the written Word of God, is much more than just another self-help/advice book, and contains the answers and wisdom they need to make the best possible decisions.
- [ ] To help kids differentiate truth from misperception in regard to what the Bible is, and to help kids understand that the Bible is for them.
- [ ] To help kids put together a plan to get more out of the Bible.
- [ ] Other ______________________________

Your Bible Base:

Psalm 119
John 5:39, 40

STEP 1

Getting Some Answers

(Needed: Fortune cookies)

OPTIONS

SMALL GROUP

LARGE GROUP

MOSTLY GUYS

EXTRA FUN

MEDIA

Have each group member think of a decision he or she needs to make soon. Some decisions may be serious concerns (what college to attend, what to major in, whether or not to join the military, etc.). Others may be quite frivolous (who to ask out this weekend, what color of jacket to buy, whether or not to go swimming this evening, etc.). Have everyone write down his or her dilemma. Then hand out fortune cookies. Say (tongue in cheek): **We're going to try to get some answers for your questions today. These fortune cookies contain excellent advice, and your job will be to apply the wisdom of your fortune cookie to your specific question.**

Let everyone open the cookies and struggle to make sense of what is written there. Have some volunteers share their decisions and fortunes, and then explain how the advice of the cookie applies to their concern. In many cases there is not likely to be any kind of direct application, which is OK. In such cases, have kids *force* some kind of connection. If the person can't come up with anything on his or her own, let other group members help stretch the meaning of the fortune to answer the question—in bizarre ways if necessary. (Creative people will make *some* kind of connection.)

Afterward, ask: **Are you ready to make your decision now? Why or why not?** Perhaps some of your group members selected situations they had already made up their minds about, and will be willing to make a decision. Most kids, however, will probably express how ludicrous it would be to act based on the musings of a fortune cookie.

Ask: **If you're not yet ready, what will need to happen before you *will be* ready to make a decision?** Let group members respond. Their answers should provide a number of sources they go to for advice—asking friends or parents, doing research in books or other media, consulting advice columns, and so forth. Considering the setting, some are likely to include "pray about it" or "see what the Bible has to say" as options. If so, press to see how they think the Bible might apply to each of the decisions they are struggling with. But don't take too long at this point. Group members will have an opportunity later in the session to put together a more complete plan to apply the Bible to their daily decisions.

STEP
2

Supply and (Too Little) Demand

(Needed: Copies of Repro Resource 1)

Hand out copies of "The Parable of the Benevolent Scientist" (Repro Resource 1). Give group members a few minutes to read the parable.

Then ask: **What do you think of the man who had a valuable and needed resource at his disposal, yet didn't use it? Why?**

How do you think the scientist must have felt to have his great invention ignored?

Since this is a parable, it must be symbolic of something else. What do you think this story might be trying to tell us? (We have God's Word at our disposal, yet we frequently choose to ignore it while we try to solve problems and find answers by our own efforts.)

How do you think God feels when He sees us stumbling around in the "garbage" of sin and confusion, rejecting all of the resources He has given us?

Why do you think so many people—especially young people—aren't more committed to searching the Bible for answers to their questions? (The language is too difficult to understand [this issue is dealt with in Session 3 of this book]; they don't know how to use the Bible to find specific help; they already suspect the Bible will conflict with what they *want* to do, and they don't want to confirm their suspicions; they don't actually believe [or care] that the Bible is God's Word; etc.)

Try to deal with each of the issues named by group members. But quickly bring the focus back to *your* group rather than young people as a whole. If other people don't want to use or believe the Bible, we can't be responsible. Yet we *are* accountable for our own knowledge and use (or lack of use) of God's written Word.

Ask: **What are your personal complaints about using the Bible? What questions do you have about how to use the Bible, or about its reliability?** Encourage group members to be completely honest about their feelings toward Bible study and their current levels of involvement. If they don't express themselves honestly, there is little hope for their getting past the problem to try some solutions that might help.

OPTIONS

STEP 3

A Long-Playing Psalm

(Needed: Bibles, chalkboard and chalk or newsprint and marker)

OPTIONS

Explain: **We may not get much out of Bible study until we begin to understand exactly how important the Bible is. It's not like Aesop's Fables, even though it contains many stories with moral points. It's not merely like Shakespeare, even though it contains much "classic" literature. It's not simply like *Bartlett's Quotations*, even though it is quoted perhaps more than any other book. The most important thing about the Bible is that it's God's Word that has been recorded for us. When we read the Bible, it's as if God is speaking to us. So using the Bible shouldn't be a boring or dreaded task. Rather than seeing it as a reference book with little practical application, we should see it as a love letter from Someone who cares about us more than anyone else ever will. It's something we need to cherish and read for the sheer thrill rather than from a mere sense of obligation.**

To help group members see how high a regard we should have for God's Word, have everyone turn to Psalm 119. (If some group members are in the habit of sharing Bibles or letting other people look up the passages, be sure each individual has a Bible and the opportunity to interact with Scripture during this exercise.) Explain that when God's Word begins to mean something to us personally, we are more likely to devote more time to reading it.

Give a little background to explain the uniqueness of this particular psalm. It's not identified as one of David's psalms, but the author has a tremendous respect for the Word of God. It is certainly the longest psalm, partially because it is written in an acrostic form. More specifically, each of the first eight verses begins with the first letter of the Hebrew alphabet. The next eight verses each begin with the second Hebrew letter. And each consecutive set of eight verses work their way in the same manner through the entire Hebrew alphabet of 22 letters (22 x 8 = 176 verses total). Throughout the entire psalm, the author continually turns his focus to the importance of God's Word.

Ask: **As you look through this psalm, what are some of the words used as synonyms for God's Word?** The following are several possible answers (interpreted from the original Hebrew, taken from *The Bible Knowledge Commentary* [Victor]):

• Law—Denotes direction or instruction
• Word—A general term for God's revelation
• Saying—A synonym for "word"
• Command(ment)—A definite, authoritative instruction
• Statutes (translated as *decrees*)—Literally, "things inscribed," referring to enacted laws
• Judgment—A judicial decision that sets a precedent; a binding law
• Precepts—A poetical word for injunctions
• Testimony (translated as *statutes*)—A solemn declaration of the will of God
• Way—A metaphor to describe a pattern of life marked out by God's Law
• Path—Similar to "way"

After group members have listed several words, ask: **Why do you think so many different words were used?** (The different words used reveal a variety of purposes of Scripture.)

Point out that God's Word contains laws and commandments that should be obeyed regardless of how we feel, but it also is a way and a path to help us feel safe, protected, and secure. We should *want* to do what God says rather than do so simply out of obligation. Another term not included on the previous list, yet that sharp-eyed group members might discover is *promise* (vs. 140, for example), or *righteous promise* (vs. 123). The Bible is more than a bunch of rules and regulations. It reveals the many things that God has in store for those who choose to follow Him.

Since Psalm 119 is too lengthy to study completely, assign groups (or individuals) random sets of eight verses each to examine. Ask each group to report on what can be gained from a better understanding of God's Word, the Bible. Psalm 119 contains several great themes: God's Word as a lamp and light (vs. 105); the "sweet" taste of God's words (vs. 103); the importance of young people living according to the Word of God (vs. 9); the strength we receive from Scripture during turbulent times (vss. 25-32); etc. As the groups report their findings, compile a master list on the board to show what an ongoing devotion through Bible study has to offer your group members.

STEP 4

Just Words on a Page

OPTIONS

Now that you've covered some of the things that the Bible *is*, spend a bit of time considering what it *isn't*. Begin by reading a number of statements and letting group members respond to them. Kids should stand if they feel a statement is true and sit if they think it is false. Here are some statements you might use:

- **The Bible is the most important book in the world.**
- **Christianity and the church would quickly deteriorate without the Bible.**
- **The Bible is a holy book and should be treated with the utmost respect.**
- **A good knowledge of the Bible ensures a good relationship with God.**
- **It's impossible to succeed in life without knowing a lot about the Bible.**
- **The Bible contains a lot of good suggestions for how people should live.**
- **Somewhere in the Bible you can find an answer to every problem you have.**

These are all broad statements. Kids' responses will probably depend on how they interpret each statement. In several cases, both "true" and "false" answers can be supported. For example, the Bible certainly contains a lot of material about how people should live, but some kids could argue (justifiably) that such things are *commands* rather than *suggestions*. The Bible might be the most important book in the world, but it won't be the most important book in the world *to us* unless we know more about it than we do any of our textbooks or favorite novels. Try to show through this exercise that some of the things we assume about the Bible may not be as black and white as we may think.

After some discussion, present a final true-false statement: **Diligent study of the Bible leads to eternal life.** Let kids respond.

Then have someone read aloud John 5:39, 40. Ask: **What do you think Jesus is trying to tell us in these verses?** It is important to see that *knowledge* of biblical truth is of little use unless it leads to *application* of that truth. God's Word should lead us to God Himself. Knowledge of Scripture is not the key to the kingdom. Jesus alone is the way, the truth, and the life (John 14:6).

Ask: **What if you really liked someone and wanted to estab-**

lish a relationship, but you never actually made personal contact with the person? You write letters and talk on the phone every once in a while, yet you never make any effort to get together in person. How strong do you think that relationship would be? How long do you think it would last? Point out that a relationship with a living God is not likely to grow or flourish if we try to relate to His Word without relating to Him personally. If we don't apply what we read in Scripture, it does us little more good than a fortune cookie. Even "diligent" study of the Bible is not enough. The Bible isn't a magical book that will take care of our problems simply because we read words on a page. But as we learn to identify principles from Bible passages and apply those principles to our own lives, our knowledge of Scripture will draw us closer to God.

STEP 5

Word Study

(Needed: Copies of Repro Resource 2)

Few topics are discussed as frequently in Christian youth groups as the importance of Bible study. Yet one reason for the recurring theme is that it's relatively easy to *discuss* the topic in a group without getting around to *doing* much about it as individuals. "What Does the Bible Say about the Bible?" (Repro Resource 2) is a "get started" resource for kids to take home. It contains a list of ten passages that deal with the importance of the Word of God and/or Bible study. Hand out a copy to each person. Ask kids to read and think about one (or more) of the passages each day during the next week. If many of your kids already have a daily devotional routine, don't have them interfere with it. But for those who don't have a regular time alone with God through His Word, have them agree to select one of the passages to do each day during the following week. Every day they will get a new insight into the value and significance of God's Word. Then at the next meeting, provide an opportunity for kids to ask questions they had during the week. You may also want to have ready another resource for daily Bible study by next week to encourage group members to continue what they start this week.

Close with a prayer of thanks to God for His written Word, as well as for Jesus, the Word who became flesh (a concept also included on the take-home Repro Resource). Ask for wisdom as group members prepare to look into the truths of Scripture during the next week.

OPTIONS

- EXTRA ACTION
- SMALL GROUP
- LITTLE BIBLE BACKGROUND
- MEDIA
- URBAN
- JR. HIGH / HIGH SCHOOL COMBINED
- EXTRA CHALLENGE

THE PARABLE OF THE BENEVOLENT SCIENTIST

Once upon a time there was a scientist who was devoted to helping people. Each day as he went to work, he would see hungry and homeless people who begged for food. He wished that no one had to go to bed hungry, so he set about inventing something that would help. Eventually he discovered a way to rearrange certain kinds of molecules, so that he could actually manufacture food out of microscopic particles contained in the air. And rather than rush to write scientific papers about his miraculous invention or go on talk shows to get famous, he instead chose to give away his new device to someone who really needed it.

On his way to work the next day, he took his pocket-sized invention with him. A man stood on the corner with a "Will Work for Food" sign, so the scientist stopped and asked if he was hungry. "I'm starving," the man said. "I haven't had anything substantial in almost a week."

The scientist smiled, handed the man the device, and explained how it worked. "All you do," he said, "is press the button to get the food you want. Here's a list with a thousand different possibilities, including chicken soup, T-bone steaks, angel hair pasta with pesto sauce, double cheeseburgers, fries, hot fudge sundaes, and just about anything else you can think of. Just key in the number of whatever you want, and the food appears."

The man on the street hit the numbers for ham, eggs over easy, hash browns, and coffee. Each item appeared in turn. The man devoured the food on the spot, and was shocked beyond words when the scientist insisted that he keep the device. The scientist then continued on to work, prepared to create another device and write out the instructions so the machines could be mass produced to feed the hungry people of the world. He was still working on his second model two weeks later when, on the way to work, he saw the guy he had given the first device to. The man was back on the streets; begging for food.

The scientist was dismayed. He stopped and asked the man, "What's wrong? Did the food device malfunction? Did you lose it? Was it stolen?"

"No," answered the man. "I still have it, and it works fine. It's back in the alley in a shopping cart with all of my other possessions."

"Then why are you out here begging for food?" asked the kind scientist.

"Well, I tried most of the things that the machine can manufacture, and it's some of the most delicious stuff I've ever eaten. But it just seems too easy to press a button and get whatever I want. Sometimes I'd just rather try to do things myself, you know? When I go through garbage cans or ask people for food, I never know what I'm going to get. Like last month I found the remains of a bucket of chicken. It must have been pretty old, because I was sick for about a week after eating it. But it was satisfying to take care of myself. Your machine makes it too easy."

The scientist walked away, disappointed. He never made another machine. Instead, he went into the field of behavioral psychology to try to understand what makes people act in such strange ways. The hungry man is still hungry. Meanwhile, the scientist's machine is still out there somewhere—lying unused in an alley or perhaps collecting dust on someone's coffee table.

WHAT DOES THE BIBLE SAY ABOUT THE BIBLE?

Most people could stand to know a little more than they do about the Bible. Sometimes it seems that the more we learn about God's Word, the less we actually know. Even though we may be aware of many of the stories and key verses, there's still a lot of material that escapes our notice.

Below is a list of passages that no one should miss. You've probably seen most of them before, but if so, take a closer look at them this time. Each one should tell you a little more about the Bible itself—and the importance of reading and studying it more often. There are ten passages. Don't do them all at once. In fact, don't read more than one a day. Then spend whatever time you have left *thinking* about what each one says.

After you read each passage, answer the following questions:

- Are any symbols used to describe God's Word? (Some passages may not have any.)
- What can you learn about the Bible (the Word of God) from this passage?
- How can you apply what this passage says to your own life? Be specific.
- What questions come to mind as you read and think about the passage? (Write them down for later discussion, even if you eventually figure out the answer on your own.)

Here are your assignments. Take your time each day and see what you can learn.

DAY 1: PROVERBS 30:5, 6

DAY 2: ISAIAH 55:8-11

DAY 3: JEREMIAH 23:25-29

DAY 4: MATTHEW 4:1-4

DAY 5: MARK 4:1-20

DAY 6: JOHN 1:1-14

DAY 7: EPHESIANS 6:10-17

DAY 8: II TIMOTHY 3:12-17

DAY 9: HEBREWS 4:12

DAY 10: JAMES 1:22-25

EXTRA ACTION

Step 3
Bring several index cards. On each card, write one of the following objects that are used in the Bible as symbols for God's Word: *lamp* (Psalm 119:105), *mirror* (James 1:23), *sword* (Hebrews 4:12), *rain* (Isaiah 55:10, 11), *snow* (Isaiah 55:10, 11), *fire* (Jeremiah 23:29), *hammer* (Jeremiah 23:29), *seed* (Mark 4:14), etc. Also throw in a few other words that sound like potential answers (*flowers*, *gavel*, *ocean*, *broom*, etc.) and some just for fun (*banana*, *Corvette*, *porcupine*, etc). Have kids form teams. You'll need one set of cards for each team. Have the teams line up on one side of the room. Place the cards on the other side. At your signal, the first person in each line will run to his or her team's pile of cards and separate them according to which ones are authentic symbols of God's Word and which aren't. After each person separates the cards, you will announce how many are incorrect. Then the next person on each team will run to the pile of cards and makes changes. Continue until one team correctly separates all of its cards.

Step 5
Point out that the Bible contains plenty of action if we simply do what it says. To demonstrate, select a group member to lead a "Bible aerobics workout." Perhaps your kids can think of several "active" biblical instructions. If not, several are listed below. Spend a few minutes performing each action as if in an aerobics class. (But don't let anyone feel uncomfortable if he or she is out of shape. Keep the mood light.) Here are some activities to use:
- *"Keep in step* with the Spirit" (Galatians 5:25)—Walk briskly around the room.
- *"Run* . . . the race marked out for us" (Hebrews 12:1)—Jog in place.
- *"Strengthen* your feeble arms and weak knees" (Hebrews 12:12)—Do pushups or knee bends.
- *"Flee* the evil desires of youth" (II Timothy 2:22)—Run around the room.
- *"Fight* the good fight of the faith" (I Timothy 6:12)—Shadow box.

SMALL GROUP

Step 1
Rather than limiting your opening activity to fortune cookies, let each group member represent a different source of advice. One person might represent a gypsy fortune teller. Others might represent a palm reader, an advice columnist, a phrenologist (someone who interprets the shape of a person's skull and bumps on the head), a parent, and a youth leader. Have each person come up with an actual decision that needs to be made, as instructed in the session. But then everyone else should provide advice (in character) for that decision. Kids may also want to demonstrate the underlying motivations for certain advice givers (money for fortune tellers, popularity for advice columnists, etc.). Afterward, ask: **How good was the advice you received? What problems arise when you seek advice from people you don't know well? In light of these potential problems, why do you think so many people are drawn to fortune tellers, astrology, and so forth?**

Step 5
Rather than hand out Repro Resource 2, which contains ten days' worth of Bible studies, create a phone chain instead. Call one group member each day and give him or her the day's Bible study passage. He or she should then call one person and pass on the information. This chain should continue until all group members have received the information. [NOTE: This may take some advance planning—exchanging phone numbers, deciding on who calls whom, etc.] An advantage of this system is that no one can claim to forget about his or her devotional time or lose the sheet that contains the day's passage. In addition, a phone chain will get your young people talking to one another. Perhaps they might begin to discuss the passages and applications from earlier in the week. But if not, at least they will have the opportunity to build fellowship while discussing things other than church and youth group.

LARGE GROUP

Step 1
Rather than dealing with individual decisions, think of a decision that would affect the entire group. It should be phrased so that it can be answered either yes or no. ("Should we disband this group so that you have more time to do homework?" "Should we give up all the fun stuff in our meetings and just have Bible studies?" "Should we take over the church and make the older people do what we want?") Have kids form teams. Assign each team a method to determine a response (either yes or no) for the decision. For example, one team might toss a coin, with heads indicating yes and tails indicating no. Another team could spin a game spinner, with an even number indicating yes and an odd number indicating no. Another team might throw dice to reach a decision. Be creative in your methods. After you ask the question, let teams use their methods to determine the answer. Try to show how ludicrous it is to use such methods to make decisions. Also point out that such things are "detestable" to God if they are taken seriously (Deuteronomy 18:10-12). When we have the Bible as a source of wisdom, it is more than foolish to use other methods of decision making—it is sinful as well.

Step 3
With a large group, you can cover *all* of Psalm 119. Divide the twenty-two sections of the psalm among your kids. As they read their assigned verses, they should prepare to answer the following questions:
- **What words are used in this passage to describe God's Word?**
- **What instructions are we given?**
- **What promises are we given?**

Discuss each of the questions as a large group, letting individuals respond. Not all of the sections will contain answers to each question, but all kids will be able to contribute frequently. Afterward, point out how much the author of the psalm was influenced by God's Word. Challenge your kids to become involved with the Bible so it will become important to them as well.

Step 2
If hearing has ceased to be effective with your group, try sight and smell to help get across a point. Prior to the meeting, set up a table of delicious-looking food in the room. As group members read the parable on Repro Resource 1, you might stroll over to the table and help yourself to what's there. You can also use the food on hand as examples of what the device in the parable could manufacture (eating as you describe). But don't allow group members to sample anything. Continue the session with the food in their presence. Only when the session draws to a conclusion and you begin to emphasize the importance of personal interaction with God's Word should you allow them to have some personal interaction with the food at hand.

Step 3
Before beginning the Bible study, ask: **How would your life be affected if it could suddenly be proven that the laws of mathematics were not actually true? What if certain portions of history were shown to be different than how they have been described to you?** (While certain classes or homework assignments might need to be adapted, little if any personal regret is likely to take place.) Then ask: **How would your life be affected if the Bible were proven to be wrong? What changes would you expect to make?** Let several kids respond. Group members' responses are likely to reflect to what extent they depend on the Bible as a source of wisdom and a moral base. Continue: **How do you know the Bible isn't wrong?** Try to help kids see that the Bible shouldn't be just another book someone forces us to read and know. Help them understand that when we don't study the Scriptures on a regular basis, *we* are the ones who will ultimately suffer.

Step 3
To introduce the importance of Bible study, play a recording of Amy Grant's "Thy Word" (from the album *Straight Ahead,* © 1983 Meadowgreen Music Co./ Bug & Bear Music). The song is based on Psalm 119:105 and is a natural lead-in to the Bible study. After playing the song, ask: **Do you think the songwriter ever dreaded Bible study? Explain. According to the lyrics, what are some of the benefits of Bible study?** (Security of knowing God is near; courage; fellowship with God; remembrance of God's love; guidance.) **How is the writer's attitude toward Bible study similar to or different from yours?**

Step 5
For a group with little Bible background, you should try to eliminate all possible reluctance group members might have to getting personally involved with the Bible. So after you hand out copies of Repro Resource 2, spend some time helping group members locate all of the references and write down the page numbers from their individual Bibles. This shouldn't take too long when done as a group, and it might remove a potential barrier for kids during the week. While it certainly would not be much trouble for someone to look up the books in a table of contents if necessary, the ease of having the page numbers available might make a difference for some kids.

Step 3
After studying Psalm 119, let kids create their own acrostic thanksgiving/praise psalm. (You may want to have them work in small groups to accomplish this.) Their psalm can take any form they wish. It need not be 176 verses, nor consist of rhyming couplets. (Though if they want to challenge themselves in such ways, they should certainly give it a try.) Perhaps the easiest form would be to create a song/prayer in which each line begins with a different letter of the alphabet. For example:
All praise we give to God
Because of His wonderful love
Creator, shepherd, and loving Father
Defender of His people and giver of
Everything we need.

Some letters of the alphabet will probably be difficult for kids to use, but don't let them get discouraged. They should simply move on to the next letter and see how many they can use. Let them create their own rules as they go along, and they may surprise you with what they come up with.

Step 4
Explain that the Bible is only effective to the extent that we do what it says. In most cases, kids will know quite a bit about what the Bible says, so try to move them to the next level—*application.* Don't force anyone to do this, but encourage volunteers to fill in this sentence: "Because God's Word says _________, I will try harder to ________." Specifically, it would be good for these statements to be directed to other group members or the group as a whole. If your goal is to build fellowship, a good starting point is the verbal affirmation to change for the better. Kids might express a need for improved levels of forgiveness, support, love, respect, or any number of other things. Then, as you continue to study the Bible in future meetings, keep coming back to this fill-in statement. Point out that any time we know something about the Bible, that knowledge should call for action on our part.

MOSTLY GIRLS

Step 2
If none of your girls mentions that there are few women highlighted in the Bible, raise this issue yourself. Ask: **Why do you think women are focused on so little in the Bible?** (The events in the Bible occurred in a patriarchal, male-dominated society.) **Does this fact make it more difficult for you to relate to the Bible? Why or why not? If you could change one thing about the Bible, what would it be? Why?**

Step 3
Many of your girls may never have thought of the Bible as something fun or interesting to read. Talk for a few minutes about the types of books your group members *do* like to read. Then make a list of what it is about those books they like. This list will likely include elements such as good stories, romance, interesting people and places, action, adventure, mystery, etc. After you've completed the list, go through the elements one at a time and try to think of parts of the Bible that contain the same elements. Your girls may be surprised to learn just how much "good stuff" the Bible contains.

MOSTLY GUYS

Step 1
One fortune cookie apiece may not do it for most guys. So get several dozen fortune cookies. Then, one at a time, let each guy describe what decision he needs to make, draw a cookie, and read the fortune. If possible, he should try to adapt the fortune to his problem. If he doesn't like the advice of the cookie, or if it makes no sense, he may draw another one (and keep going until he finds one he likes). Continue with various decisions until you run out of cookies. But to keep the cookies from running out too quickly, score the activity so that the person who uses the fewest cookies wins. Guys should make some attempt to apply the advice of the fortune to their problem. But if it makes no sense at all, allow them additional fortunes (and more cookies to eat).

Step 3
As you study Psalm 119, dwell on the issue of *dependence* on God's Word. Ask: **Do most guys like to admit that they have to depend on anything or anyone? Why? Even if you agree that you need to depend on the Bible, are you ever embarrassed to admit it? If so, in what situations? Do you think biblical concepts such as purity and humility are important, or is being a pain and "sowing wild oats" part of growing up if you're a guy?** Let your group members express their opinions about these issues. Then point out the clear dependence expressed by the author of the psalm. Challenge your guys not to let preoccupation with image or attitude prevent them from depending on God. Encourage them to make every effort to let God's Word help them through life.

EXTRA FUN

Step 1
Have group members form teams. Instruct each team to brainstorm several trios of things that have a common bond. For example, the trio of "angel," "cat," and "sword" have the common bond of being kinds of fish. The trio of "Black," "Enchanted," and "Sherwood" have the common bond of being names of forests. Explain that each team should write down a number of trios. The goal is to make them difficult, but not too obscure. After a few minutes, have the teams play against each other. (You will act as judge if someone claims that a particular trio of words is not logical, or if a team comes up with a correct answer that isn't the intended answer.) If you have four teams, one team will read a trio of words. The other three teams will then huddle and see if they can think of the common bond. Have the teams write down their answers. Then at your signal, have them tell you what they wrote. Keep score to see which team does best. To wrap up the activity and move to the next part of the session, give a trio of your own: **Lamp, Sword, and Mirror**. (All are words used to describe God's Word.)

Step 2
Create a play from the parable on Repro Resource 1. Write dialogue from the narrative portions wherever possible, and use a narrator for the rest. Add new characters if you wish (fellow scientists, other street people, etc.). As you put together the play, adapt it for a particular audience. It might be for your church congregation, another youth group, or a class of younger kids. Whatever the intended audience, try to make the characters and dialogue appropriate for them. As time permits, give thought to simple backgrounds you could create or props and costumes to use. If possible, group members should perform the play for another group (and be ready to explain what they've learned in this session).

OPTIONS

SESSION ONE

Step 1
Instead of using the fortune-cookie opening, tape record a number of kids asking questions about the decisions they need to make. Don't explain why you're doing it. Simply get them to share some of the decisions that loom in their future, as well as any difficulties they face in trying to make the decisions. Then as you begin the session, set up the room as a radio studio in which a call-in talk-show host has a panel of "experts" discussing decision making. One at a time, announce that you have a "caller" and play a section of the tape you made. Let your student panel try to offer the best advice possible about making the decision that is described. Afterward, have group members express whether or not the advice was helpful. Then ask: **When you need to make a major decision, what media do you use? Besides media, where do you go for help with your big choices? Which of these sources is consistently most beneficial?**

Step 5
Bring in some children's ABC books. Give kids a few minutes to look them over. Then explain that group members will be using the letters in the book to describe the Bible. Write each letter of the alphabet on a separate slip of paper. Put the slips into a container. Have each group member draw one or more slips (depending on the size of your group). Instruct each person to use the letter(s) that he or she drew to complete this sentence: "The Bible is __________" (accurate, believable, comforting, etc.). [NOTE: For information's sake, "xciting" does not qualify as a word.] After everyone has shared his or her idea(s), compile this "ABCs of the Bible" list. You may even want to photocopy it, add some artwork, and sell it to parents as a fundraiser for your group.

Step 3
With the length of Psalm 119, one option for conducting a short session is to spend the entire time studying the passage. Divide the psalm into sections. Assign each group member (or small group) a different section of the psalm to read and be prepared to talk about. Then lead the session by asking questions and letting group members respond. Start with simple questions like these: **From what you read, do you think the writer thought Bible study was valuable? How can you tell?** Then move on to specifics: **What can Bible study do for you? How can it help you during a time of stress? How can it help you when things are going really well?** Finally, spend time on personal application: **What would it take for you to get as enthused about Scripture as the writer of this psalm was? Of everything he says, what is most likely to convince you to "dig a little deeper" into the Bible? How can you prevent Bible reading from becoming monotonous and dull?**

Step 4
Begin the session with Step 4. Allow group members to express their opinions about the Bible. Then move from their opinions to the importance of Scripture—not as a magic cure-all for our woes, but as a signpost that points us to a personal relationship with God Himself. Try to generate a number of questions. Then move back to Step 3 and discuss Psalm 119 as you search for answers to the questions that have been raised. Finally, hand out Repro Resource 2 as a take-home sheet.

Step 2
Ask: **How many of you know people who try to use the latest slang or who think they know all about what's "in" as far as clothing, music, and movies are concerned—when they really haven't got a clue?** Most of your kids probably have opinions about such faux hipsters. Then ask if your kids ever think of the Bible in the same way—as something that pretends to be relevant today, but that is actually outdated. If your kids have such feelings about the Bible, it's likely that part of the reason has to do with the language of the Bible. So give your kids an opportunity to translate some of the "hard to understand" verses in the Bible into the *New Hype Version* (NHV). This NHV Bible should feature the language of the urban youth culture. Have kids form teams. Assign each team a passage of Scripture to translate. Explain that the NHV Bible will be available on videotape as well as in print, so teams should feel free to translate passages using writing, drama, music, dance, etc. After a few minutes, have each team share its translated passage.

Step 5
Before you hand out Repro Resource 2, have a few people armed with rolls of toilet paper burst into the room. They should begin wrapping anyone in their path with the toilet paper. Some of your kids may prevent the invaders from wrapping them; others may allow themselves to be wrapped. After a few minutes, the volunteers should leave. Afterward, draw a parallel between this bizarre occurrence and the Bible. Point out that once God's Word is loosed, nothing can stop it—even though some people may reject being "wrapped up" in its security. Then hand out Repro Resource 2. As your kids work on the assignment during the week, they should consider how Scripture can be "let loose" in their life to "wrap" others with God's Word.

OPTIONS

SESSION ONE

JR. HIGH / HIGH SCHOOL COMBINED

Step 2
Separate your junior highers from your high schoolers to read and discuss the parable on Repro Resource 1. Ask the questions from Step 2 while the kids are in separate groups. Then have the two groups come back together and review their answers. Compare their answers. Are they similar? Or do the members of the two age groups have different observations and perspectives? Sometimes when you have a wide diversity of age groups, the two extremes can teach each other. The younger ones can learn from the maturity of some of the older ones. And the older group members, who may be becoming jaded by some of the harsh realities of adult life, can see the simplicity of younger kids and recall the joys of childlikeness. More often, the two extremes may tend to see the worst about each other. But with a little help, they may occasionally be able to learn something from each other.

Step 5
After you hand out copies of Repro Resource 2, say: **In addition to the verses listed on the sheet, I think it would be good for us to add the verses *we* think are important.** Then ask each person to tell what his or her favorite verse is while everyone else writes down the references in a corner of the sheet. (Or, as an option, you can collect the list of verses, type them up, make copies, and provide new sheets next week.) If older group members have been devoted to Bible study and are becoming spiritually mature, they should have a variety of verses they've come across that left an impression on them. When the younger ones see this, they may be more inspired to give serious Bible study a try. But if few people can cite a verse other than John 3:16, you will have the opportunity to close with a challenge to explore other parts of the Bible individually, when God can "speak" through His Word and direct us to portions of Scripture that will give us help and hope.

EXTRA CHALLENGE

Step 3
After reading and discussing a 176-verse acrostic song, challenge group members to adapt other literary forms that will honor God. Whatever kids are studying in English class can probably be adapted: haiku (a non-rhyming poem with three lines of five, seven, and five syllables), limericks, parodies ("How do I love thee? Let me count the ways"), Dr. Seuss rhyme patterns, iambic pentameter, etc. Group members' efforts need not be long or complex—simply original and sincere. Have volunteers read what they create.

Step 5
Frequently when young people discuss the importance of Scripture, questions arise about how we got the Bible and why we should trust it more than any other book. It is difficult to answer all such questions quickly, so it may be wise to schedule a follow-up session to deal exclusively with matters of canonicity and authenticity. One of the best ways to deal with the questions is to provide young people with good (understandable) resources and let *them* do a bit of research. As you wrap up this session, you might want to have group members brainstorm some initial questions they have. Then find some volunteers willing to look for specific answers to these questions. While new questions are likely to arise when you get into a full-scale discussion, at least you'll provide a starting point and get your young people involved.

PLANNING CHECKLIST

Date Used:

Approx. Time

Step 1: Getting Some Answers ______
o Small Group
o Large Group
o Mostly Guys
o Extra Fun
o Media

Step 2: Supply and (Too Little) Demand ______
o Heard It All Before
o Mostly Girls
o Extra Fun
o Urban
o Combined Jr. High/High School

Step 3: A Long-Playing Psalm ______
o Extra Action
o Large Group
o Heard It All Before
o Little Bible Background
o Fellowship & Worship
o Mostly Girls
o Mostly Guys
o Short Meeting Time
o Extra Challenge

Step 4: Just Words on a Page ______
o Fellowship & Worship
o Short Meeting Time

Step 5: Word Study ______
o Extra Action
o Small Group
o Little Bible Background
o Media
o Urban
o Combined Jr. High/High School
o Extra Challenge

SESSION 2

What a Bunch of Characters!

YOUR GOALS FOR THIS SESSION:

Choose one or more

- [ ] To help kids see that the Bible is essentially one long story—not just a random collection of short stories about a variety of interesting characters.
- [ ] To help kids begin to piece together some of the stories they know to see how the stories interrelate.
- [ ] To have kids interview Christians they know to see how those people—as well as the kids themselves—are part of the ongoing story of God's redemption of the world.
- [ ] Other ______________________________

____

Your Bible Base:

Hebrews 11:32–12:3

STEP 1

The Piece That Passes Understanding

(Needed: Jigsaw puzzle [completed and broken into sections], envelopes, team prize [optional])

OPTIONS

Prior to the meeting, find a jigsaw puzzle that won't take too long to assemble, yet will present a bit of a challenge for your group members. First assemble the puzzle and then break it into sections that are approximately the same size. (Choose a number of sections that will correspond to the number of groups you wish to form during the meeting. So if your group usually breaks into four smaller groups for discussion, Bible study, and so forth, break the puzzle into fourths.) Keep the sections of the puzzle separated. Then mix the pieces within each section, placing the sections in individual envelopes. But before you do, take one key piece from the center of each section and put it in a *different* envelope. So each group will be missing one crucial piece of its section of puzzle and will have one piece that just doesn't fit at all.

At the beginning of the session, have kids form groups. Explain that you're going to have a contest to see which group can assemble its puzzle first. You might want to announce that the winning group will receive a prize (perhaps a bag of candy) if you think it will bring out the competitive nature of your group members. At your signal, groups should open their envelopes and begin to assemble their puzzle pieces.

It shouldn't take groups long to discover they have a "wrong" piece. Astute groups should also see that they have only a portion of the whole puzzle. They might want to "make a trade" with another group to complete the individual sections. Groups who figure this out should share the prize. Finally, have all of the groups combine their portions of the puzzle to see the complete picture.

Afterward, ask: **Did you ever work really hard to put a jigsaw puzzle together, only to discover at the end that a piece or two was missing? If so, how did you feel?**

When you put together jigsaw puzzles, is it more enjoyable when you're first starting or when you have only a small portion to go? Why? (It's usually easy to put together the "frame" or border of outside pieces. Then it becomes difficult to assemble the interior until there are only a few pieces left.)

Does the Bible ever seem like a "puzzle" to you? If so, in what ways? Many groups frequently deal with "puzzling" teachings of the Bible. This time, however, stress the importance of putting together individual pieces of Bible knowledge. Most young people know selected stories and assorted key passages, but we need to keep "working at the puzzle" until we can see how it *all* fits together. Missing pieces should frustrate us just the same as with a jigsaw puzzle.

STEP 2

Good Connections

(Needed: Copies of Repro Resource 3, pencils)

Hand out copies of "What's the Connection?" (Repro Resource 3) and pencils. Let group members see how many "connections" they can make between some of the primary characters in the Bible. If your group members have a good understanding of the Bible (or if you want to review something you've recently studied), have them add some lesser-known characters to their sheets. When they finish, have them add up the lines they drew and see who came up with the most connections.

Afterward, single out a few of the characters on the sheet and ask: **Who did you connect this person to?**

Some of the basic connections are as follows:

1. Adam—Eve—Cain—Abel
2. Abraham—Sarah—Isaac—Jacob—Esau—Judah
3. Moses—Aaron—Miriam—Pharaoh—Joshua—Caleb
4. Deborah—Gideon—Samson
5. Ruth—Naomi—Boaz
6. Elijah—Ahab—Jezebel—Elisha
7. David—Bathsheba—Solomon—Absalom
8. Isaiah—Daniel—Micah—Jonah—Hosea
9. Jesus—Peter—Andrew—Pilate—Barabbas—Nicodemus—Woman at the Well
10. Paul—Silas—Timothy—Titus—Philemon

Most of these connections refer to family members or associates of the key person listed first. Consequently, many of the names that follow are related to each other as well. In a couple of instances, the connections involve job responsibility. (For example, all of the people for #4 are judges; all of the people for #8 are prophets.) Many connections can be made between numbers as well. For example, Boaz, David, and Jesus could all be connected to Judah since they were from his tribe. Paul encountered a post-resurrection Jesus on the road to Damascus and

OPTIONS

made references to Abraham, Moses, and others. And in a sense, all of the characters could be connected to Adam and Eve. Any connections your group members can make (and substantiate) should be accepted.

After group members total and discuss the connections they made between characters, use the groupings to review some of the basic periods of biblical history: Creation, the Patriarchs, Bondage and Deliverance, Judges, Kings, Captivity and the Prophets, the Life of Jesus, and the Formation and Continuation of the Church. Point out that as complex as it may seem from the number of stories and characters involved, the Bible is actually an ongoing account of God's relationship with humankind. That relationship began in perfection; then we sinned and distanced ourselves from God. But God forgave us and provided a way back to Him. And the Bible has a happy ending with God's people restored to full and perfect fellowship with Him.

Ask: **Why do you think the Bible contains so many stories about people? Wouldn't it be a lot shorter if God simply gave us a list of dos and don'ts and skipped all of the personal anecdotes?** Spend some time letting group members think about this. Among other things, they should discover that

- characters give the Bible a sense of history (the Persian kings, Augustus Caesar, etc.)
- through character studies we see *consequences* of obedience and rebellion
- we tend to relate better to people than to rules and regulations
- God is more concerned in the *application* of the "dos and don'ts" than in our simply knowing them.

STEP 3

We're Being Watched

(Needed: Bibles)

Ask: **Other than Jesus, who is your favorite Bible character? Why?** Let several group members respond.

Then ask: **Where in the Bible do you turn to read about your favorite character?** See if most of your group members can provide a quick reference. If not, perhaps some of them are drawing on stories they've *heard,* but haven't actually *read* in quite a while. Then explain that there is one place in the Bible where many of their chosen characters—Old Testament ones, anyway—are mentioned in the same place. Have group members turn to Hebrews 11 and skim the chapter to see if they find the characters they chose. Some may be named specifically. Others may be alluded to in the latter verses of the chapter.

Have someone read aloud Hebrews 11:32-38. Then ask: **Who do you think some of these unnamed people might be?** Any number of answers may be correct. For example, Solomon administered justice; Daniel withstood the lions' den; Deborah was a powerful judge; etc. Also note that there have been *many* people who were faithful to God in all of these ways, yet whose stories were never recorded.

Of all the sufferings mentioned here, which do you think would be most difficult to endure? Why?

What does it mean that "the world was not worthy of" the people who endured these sufferings? (They were living for God in a sinful world. In many cases, it seemed that *they* were the "losers"; but ultimately, it's only God's opinion that matters. In reality, these were exceptional people who would eventually receive great honor and rewards from God.)

Have someone read aloud Hebrews 11:39, 40. Then ask: **What had been promised to these people that they hadn't yet received?** (A Messiah who, among other things, would restore the relationship between God and His people.)

What did God plan that would be "better for us"? (He provided a Savior. Today we can examine the person and work of Jesus to see what God has done for us and how we should act. We also have the Holy Spirit actively at work in our lives.)

How many of the characters named in Hebrews lived perfect lives? (Obviously none.)

Then what was the big deal about *their* faith as opposed to ours? (They endured numerous obstacles and persevered as people of God based only on a *promise* of better things to come. They had few if any of the assurances we have today.)

Have someone read Hebrews 12:1-3. Then ask: **What should be our relationship with such faithful Old Testament characters?** (They played their roles early in God's story and "paved the way" for us. We need to acknowledge their contributions by learning all we can from them and making any needed changes in the way we live. As we heed their examples, we join them in what God desires for us [Hebrews 11:40].)

When you think of having these great people of the faith as "witnesses" of how you are currently living your life, how does it make you feel? Why?

What are some of the sins and hindrances that "entangle" many people your age? How, specifically, might they "throw off" each one?

If you sought really hard to lead a life that would please God, and if you suffered a lot along the way, how do you

OPTIONS

think you would feel if everyone just seemed to ignore you? (While we shouldn't live our lives to impress others, we might naturally hope to be good examples and influences on others. If they didn't seem to care about our dedication or the difficulties we faced, we might be somewhat disappointed or forlorn.) Point out that by learning from the examples of biblical characters, we give significance to their lives and help demonstrate that their sacrifices were not in vain.

To help show the importance of learning lessons from the lives of people recorded in the Bible, have volunteers look up and be ready to read the following pairs of passages:

- Jonah 1:17 and Matthew 12:38-41
- Genesis 19:24-28 and Luke 10:8-12
- Genesis 7:17-23 and Matthew 24:36-41

In each of these pairs, a well-known Bible story is alluded to by Jesus as He makes a point. Have group members first read both sets of verses and then explain what point Jesus was trying to make. Also explain that Jesus used both positive and negative examples from Scripture to help people understand what He was trying to say. The biblical accounts of the past were recorded to affect *our* present and future. They should be more than mere stories to us. We need to pay careful attention to the lives of those people and the lessons they can teach us.

STEP 4

Contemporary Characters

(Needed: Bibles, paper, pencils, panel of adults [optional])

Some people may work very hard to examine the lives of Bible characters and draw out practical applications they can make based on those characters' lives. Yet those same people may tend to overlook God's people *today*—alive and active in their churches. If we were to become just a bit more observant and inquisitive, we might be likely to find all kinds of stories *from people we already know* that would help us lead better Christian lives and avoid a lot of potential mistakes.

If possible, arrange to have a panel of adults from your church available to be interviewed during this part of the session. Try to select people who can give concise but striking testimonies of how God has worked in their lives. Explain that as we look back on our lives, we often get a completely different perspective than we have while we're going through the various phases. We can sometimes see reasons for the things we could never understand before. We might see a time when God said no to something we desperately wanted—only to see Him provide something better. We might see amazing ways He directs us to spouses or close friends. And we might see, in retrospect, how important our faith was during those times (and how little good our whining and complaining did).

As you introduce each member of your panel, explain one of the things you think your group members might be able to learn from the person. (One panel member might have a high-school anecdote, another might have a choosing-a-college story, another might have a romantic remembrance, etc.) Then open the floor to questions from group members. You might want to have some queries ready in case kids are slow getting started. It shouldn't take long for group members to see that God still works just as frequently and powerfully (if not *quite* as miraculously) as He did for the characters in the Bible.

Even if you don't have the opportunity to set up a panel, don't pass up the opportunity to learn from some of your fellow Christians. Instead of the panel, have individuals or small groups plan to interview some people in your church. Perhaps your kids have witnessed traits of certain members (through testimonies, prayers, ability to handle crises, etc.) that would create a desire to know those members better. If so, have them try to set up some appointments with those church members. If your kids don't know other church members well, *you* might want to suggest some potential matches (putting student athletes with former ballplayers, putting student and adult musicians together, and so forth). Then spend some time letting kids write out several questions that they would want to ask the adults. They should also be thinking of things they could reveal about themselves that would allow the adults to know them better. Do what you can to facilitate the interviews, but leave the "work" to group members. At your next meeting, let group members report back on what they learned. They might be surprised to discover to what extent God is at work among your church and its members.

OPTIONS

SMALL GROUP

FELLOWSHIP & WORSHIP

MEDIA

URBAN

JR. HIGH HIGH SCHOOL COMBINED

STEP 5

People of God: The Next Generation

(Needed: Copies of Repro Resource 4, pencils)

Summarize: **According to what we read in Hebrews, many people suffered in order for us to know more about God.**

OPTIONS

EXTRA ACTION · LARGE GROUP · JR HIGH / HIGH SCHOOL COMBINED · EXTRA CHALLENGE

We can also see God at work in the lives of people right here in our church. We have numerous books and films to show how the power of God has made profound changes in individuals and groups throughout history. But exactly what should all of this mean to us? Let group members respond. Eventually, they should see that now it's *their* turn to set good examples for others. Explain that the story of God's love for humankind didn't end with the writing of the Bible. It still continues today. Your group members are "sequels" to the stories they read in the Bible. Your group members are accountable for learning from the characters of the past, and then applying that information to their lives so *they* will become better models for people in the present and future. They can have strong influences on friends, parents, brothers and sisters, teachers, neighbors, and even total strangers.

Hand out copies of "Take a Look at Yourself" (Repro Resource 4). Have group members recall their behavior during the last week, evaluate it, and record appropriate comments. When they finish, let volunteers share some of the observations they made about themselves.

Then ask: **What would you think about having your life recorded for posterity as a story in a holy book for people to study and learn from? Would those people be more likely to learn from the times when you performed bold acts of faith, or the ones where you messed up?** Let kids respond.

Then say: **When you look at the characters in the Bible, you won't find much about their teenage years—in most cases. Even as adults, it took most of them a while to discover that God had a special purpose for them. Moses, Noah, Paul, Jesus' disciples, and Sarah are good examples of this. Other times people found God's plan for their lives, but then abandoned God's ways late in life—people such as King Saul, Solomon, and Gideon. We need to study all of these characters carefully so we can get an early start, but avoid making the same mistakes. Thanks to these characters, we know the importance of starting *now* to be faithful to God, and we can see what we have to lose if we don't *continue* to grow in our relationship with Him.**

Close with a challenge for your group members to begin dealing with any specific problem areas they've already noted on Repro Resource 4. From there, they can move on to other problems they discover in their lives. But the sooner they get started, the longer they will be able to experience the wonderful things God can do for and through them.

WHAT'S THE CONNECTION?

Sometimes the Bible may seem like just a bunch of stories about various characters. But many of those characters are connected to each other in one way or another. Look through the names below and draw a line to connect any that you know for sure have some kind of association. (No guessing! You must be able to explain the connection between the two people.)

CAIN

AARON

HOSEA

MIRIAM

SARAH

CALEB

ABEL

ISAAC

NAOMI

JOSHUA

DANIEL

ABRAHAM

ISAIAH

PAUL

DAVID

SILAS

ABSALOM

PETER

DEBORAH

JACOB

SOLOMON

ADAM

PHARAOH

ELIJAH

AHAB

JESUS

PHILEMON

TIMOTHY

ELISHA

ANDREW

JONAH

PILATE

TITUS

BARABBAS

ESAU

SAMSON

WOMAN AT THE WELL

MICAH

RUTH

BATHSHEBA

EVE

JUDAH

BOAZ

GIDEON

MOSES

JEZEBEL

NICODEMUS

TAKE A LOOK AT YOURSELF

Do you ever hear or read a Bible story and then become critical of the characters in the story? For example, do any of the following comments sound familiar?

- "Adam and Eve were in paradise, but they ate the forbidden fruit. How stupid!"
- "How dumb could Samson be to tell Delilah his secret and end up blind and imprisoned?"
- "That rich young guy could have followed Jesus, but he was just too selfish!"

Of course, it's easy to sit back and comment about the shortcomings of *other* people. But let's suppose people have been watching *your* every move for the past week. And suppose your words, thoughts, and actions were all recorded—just like those of Bible characters. After reading the story of your life during the previous week, what would someone be likely to say about the following things? (Be specific about the comments you would expect to receive.)

	Positive Comments	**Negative Comments**
Your language		
Your actions		
Your relationships (parents, friends, etc.)		
Your thoughts		
Your spiritual life		
Other miscellaneous observations		

"Don't let anyone look down on you because you are young, but set an example for the believers in speech, in life, in love, in faith and in purity" (I Timothy 4:12).

EXTRA ACTION

Step 1
To begin the session, hand out several Tinker Toys or Legos to each group member. Instruct him or her to create something unique. Be sure to reserve a few pieces for yourself because you'll need them later. If possible, have group members work around a large table so that their creations can be moved without a lot of effort. After a few minutes, have each person display his or her work and describe what it is. Then after everyone has shared, try to connect all of the individual works (using the pieces you saved for yourself) to make one large creation. Use this activity to introduce the topic of Bible characters. Though each person has a special and unique story, in reality, each one merely contributes to the single story of God's love and redemption.

Step 5
Wrap up the session with one of your group's favorite relay races—Lifesavers on toothpicks, eggs in spoons, or whatever. If your group doesn't have a favorite, try a traditional, pass-the-baton relay. The point you want to make is that just as an Olympic four-person relay depends heavily on individual contributions for the good of the team, so we all need to work hard as individuals for the good of the church. While some young people may be a little too hyperactive to absorb these truths at the end of a session, they may be more receptive after they've run the length of the room (or around the building) several times and are eager for a break.

SMALL GROUP

Step 2
Instead of using Repro Resource 2 as written, divide the characters on the sheet among your kids. Add others as needed so that each person has a list of at least five characters that no one else has. Announce a number of categories for which kids can get a certain number of points per character on their list. For instance, ask: **Can you name the parents of any of the people on your list?** If kids can name both parents, they get two points; if they can name one parent, they get one point. In some cases—such as Adam and Eve, or characters whose parents aren't mentioned—there will be no opportunity for points. But such instances should balance themselves out as you move on to other categories. Also, kids should be reasonably sure of their answers. You won't have time to look up wild guesses to see whether or not they are correct. Other categories might include the following:

- **Name a bad thing each person did.** (Maximum one point per character.)
- **Name the children of each person.** (One point per kid for each character.)
- **Quote something each person said.** (Maximum one point per character.)
- **Name the book(s) of the Bible in which you would find each character.** (One point per book for each character.)

Step 4
Instruct each of your group members to think of a Bible character and a person he or she knows (personally) who share a common trait. For instance, someone might say, "Thomas—Jesus' disciple—and my grandfather both refuse to believe that something is true until they see it with their own eyes." Award prizes for the most creative comparisons.

LARGE GROUP

Step 1
Begin the session by forming a human machine. Have group members imagine they are cogs, levers, wheels, or any other machine part. Start with one or two people performing some mechanical function, and gradually add others until you have formed one enormous machine. Be sure to add a variety of sounds as well. The more group members respond to each other's movements, the better your "machine" will be. Use your human machine to demonstrate how many parts with various functions can have a single, unified goal. Similarly, the characters described in Scripture are unique and diverse, yet contribute to the unified story of God's salvation of the world.

Step 5
Ask kids to name their favorite reading material—the types of books and magazines they most enjoy. You'll need to have available a large supply of various types of books and magazines. When a group member identifies what he or she most likes to read, hand him or her a sample of that reading material. It's likely that few, if any, of your kids will name the Bible as their favorite reading material. So after everyone has chosen a book, say: **Even though the Bible may not be our favorite thing to read, we need to make an effort to read it as regularly as possible. If we spend most of our time reading other things, the Bible can get lost in the shuffle.** To demonstrate this, place a Bible on the floor at the front of the room. Then have kids come forward one at a time to stack their book or magazine on top of the Bible. (For fun, you might see how high you can get the stack before it topples over.) Afterward, explain that it's OK to enjoy reading things other than the Bible—as long as the Bible doesn't get "lost" among them. Our first priority should be to spend time in God's Word.

HEARD IT ALL BEFORE

Step 2

After kids complete Repro Resource 3, but before you discuss it, conduct a contest. Hand out paper and pens. Ask:

- **How many stories do you think are contained in the Bible?**
- **How many commandments are there for us to follow?**

After kids have written their answers for both questions, instruct them to add the two numbers together. Then announce that the sum they should have come up with is three. Explain: **The Bible is one ongoing story that begins with God's creation of a paradise and humankind's fall, moves forward to God's plan of salvation for His fallen people, and concludes with the restoration of the relationship—at which time God and His people are together again in His paradise. Everything else in the Bible is a subplot to that one main story. And as for the commandments, Jesus narrowed them down to two for us. He said, "'Love the Lord your God with all your heart and with all your soul and with all your mind.' This is the first and greatest commandment. And the second is like it: 'Love your neighbor as yourself.' All the Law and the Prophets hang on these two commandments"** (Matthew 22:37-40). Point out that sometimes we get too involved in the emphasis on "Bible trivia" and lose the perspective of the Bible as one cohesive story.

Step 3

Emphasize how much Jesus knew about the Old Testament and how frequently He applied it to Himself and His teachings. Single out His comment about how His own experience would be like Jonah in the belly of a great fish (Matthew 12:40). Ask: **Who is your favorite Bible character? How does one of that person's experiences apply specifically to something you're currently facing?** Have volunteers share their responses.

LITTLE BIBLE BACKGROUND

Step 2

Group members without much Bible background aren't likely to know the stories of all of the characters on Repro Resource 3 (or later in the session). If they don't seem to know many of the connections for some of the characters on the sheet, take some time to help them find the source of the stories in their Bibles. You need not have them read the story at this time, but encourage them to do so sometime during the following week. Explain that the best way to cover so much material is to do a little bit each day (or *almost* every day). Point out that if we try to understand the Bible only during church and/or youth group, we are almost certain to stay confused about much of it.

Step 3

As you discuss the characters mentioned in Hebrews 11, try to determine their distinctive personalities rather than simply lumping them together as "the faithful people of the Bible." You may have to summarize some of the stories. After you do, explain: **If there had been "Faith Awards" during Bible times, these people would have been the winners. But since there weren't, which of today's awards do you think each of these people might have a chance to win?** Let group members try to think of appropriate matches between people and awards. For example, Samson might win a professional wrestler's championship belt. David, for all his psalms, might win a Grammy. Noah could win the America's Cup for sailing. Try to think of all kinds of awards, including the "Senior Superlatives" that many schools have (Most Likely to Succeed, Cutest Couple, Most Intelligent, etc.).

FELLOWSHIP & WORSHIP

Step 3

During a study on the importance of knowing Scripture, the temptation may be to keep the discussion on an academic level. But since this session focuses on the vast assortment of human characters described in the Bible, you have a good opportunity to focus on fellowship. After going through the passage in Hebrews 11, have each group member focus on one Bible character that he or she finds particularly interesting, and complete this sentence: "I really appreciate __________ because he (or she) __________." Then have kids complete the same sentence using each other's names. Go from person to person as the rest of the group expresses reasons for appreciation. You should participate as well. Be prepared to express appreciation for kids who may be overlooked by others. Try to help everyone feel affirmed during this activity. As God's servants in the present and future, group members should feel just as important as His servants of the past.

Step 4

If you can't assemble a panel of adults to interview, at least recognize the ones who have influenced your kids. Ask each group member to make a list of the adults who have been most influential in modeling faith. Each person's list should contain as many names as he or she can think of. After kids finish their lists, have them write a brief note to each person on the list, explaining why he or she has been influential in the young person's life. If you're short on time, come up with a single sentiment that can be copied and sent to everyone on your kids' lists. For instance, you might write "Your name was mentioned by our group members as someone whose outstanding faith and lifestyle is an inspiration to us." Then *everyone* can sign each card before you send them out. Your kids may be surprised at how much a small token of appreciation like this can mean to adults who are struggling to lead good Christian lives in today's world.

MOSTLY GIRLS

Step 2
The end of this step offers a good opportunity to talk about the fact that though the Bible contains more stories of men than of women, it is—from cover to cover—a book about relationships, especially God's relationship with us. Point out that the keys and principles of relationships know no gender bounds. Ask: **What are some ingredients—good or bad—of a relationship that can be found in stories in the Bible?** List these ingredients on the board as your group members name them. After you've listed several ingredients, discuss which of your girls' relationships have similar qualities.

Step 3
Have each of your girls choose a female character from the Bible whom she admires and would like to know more about. If your girls have trouble coming up with a character, offer some of the following ones to choose from: Sarah, Ruth, Esther, Mary, Elizabeth, Martha, etc. (Add some of your own favorite characters to the list.) After your girls have chosen their character, ask volunteers to share which character they chose and explain why they chose her. Challenge your group members to do a little digging in the Bible this week to see what else they can learn about the character they chose.

MOSTLY GUYS

Step 2
After completing Repro Resource 3, have group members list all of the female Bible characters they can think of who set a positive example. Then go through the list character by character. Ask: **What can we learn from the life of this woman?** If none of your guys mention them, point out the following facts:

• There are many positive female examples in the Bible—Sarah, Hannah, Deborah, Jael, the woman at the well, the woman who anointed Jesus' feet, Mary, Ruth, Esther, Lydia, and many others.
• Even so, the accounts of men greatly outnumber those of women.
• The faithful examples set by these women aren't just for other women; guys should learn from such examples as well.

After making these observations, discuss the importance of seeing similar examples in the lives of female *peers*. Challenge your guys to begin to deal with any gender bias they may be developing. If nowhere else, they should strive to set aside any potential for discrimination while at church and youth group.

Step 3
Guys are sometimes reluctant to apply what they learn in Scripture to their own lives. Help them deal with this tendency by getting them to associate with the *feelings* of some of their Bible heroes. Ask: **Which Old Testament character are you most like? Why?** Or ask: **Which of Jesus' disciples are you most like? Why?** Then ask some follow-up questions to get your guys thinking about what the person actually experienced. So if someone replies, "Daniel," ask: **If it had been you standing in front of King Darius, knowing that to admit you were praying would lead to almost certain death, what would you have done?** Try to show your guys that faith is rarely as simple as we sometimes assume. It takes great courage and strength to stand firmly for God when to do so makes us unpopular or otherwise at risk.

EXTRA FUN

Step 1
Rather than using the jigsaw-puzzle opening, try a storytelling activity. Designate someone to begin a story, making it up as he or she goes along. (Some of the best stories will include members of your group.) Before the storyteller gets too far into the plot, stop the person and designate someone else to take over. Keep letting various people take over the storytelling responsibilities until you finally ask someone to end the tale. While many such stories are not likely to make a lot of sense, use this fact to demonstrate that the Bible is really one long story—and it makes a lot more sense than the story your group came up with.

Step 2
Assign each group member the identity of a Bible character. Then give kids five minutes to find as many other characters in the room as possible who have something in common with their character. Common characteristics might include things like being discussed in the same book of the Bible, being a witness to a miracle of God, etc. (Being male or female is *not* good enough to qualify as an acceptable common trait.) After five minutes, have group members share the common characteristics they found.

MEDIA

Step 1
Before the session, collect a variety of images of cartoon characters—either in print or on video. (Some characters should be rather obscure, but not too unreasonable.) Also collect several pictures of Bible characters, using whatever preschool or primary art you can find—or perhaps an illustrated Bible story book. First, have a contest to see who can identify the most cartoon characters. After determining a winner, try it again—this time with the Bible characters. But when you show the characters, cover up any hints that would indicate who the person is. (Noah should be seen without an ark or animals; David should be seen without Goliath; etc.) Again determine a winner. Afterward, discuss how important a specific identity is to cartoon characters. Their creators don't want them to be confused with other characters. Yet sometimes when we think of Bible characters, we picture them as being rather generic (physically, at least). Therefore, we need to study their stories carefully so that we can easily differentiate Moses from Abraham and Noah, and Ruth from Esther and Mary. To lump them all together into the images we recall from childhood is to miss out on their most important individual contributions.

Step 4
If you have a video camera available, consider shooting an "appreciation video" for the church as a whole. Put together a rough script of what various group members want to say. Some might express appreciation to specific people for specific reasons; others might thank the church as a whole. Explain that you will try to find an opportunity for the adults of the church to watch the video, so group members should make sure no one feels overlooked. Then find a way for the adults in your church to see what your group members put together—perhaps during the church service, at a congregational meeting, or (on a rotating basis) in various adult Sunday School classes and Bible studies.

SHORT MEETING TIME

Step 1
Before the meeting, find a chart or timeline that summarizes Bible history. (The Good Things Company [Drawer N, Norman, Oklahoma 73070] offers a very detailed family tree of Jesus that would work well.) Place the chart in a central location and let it be the center of your meeting. First, have group members point out all of the names they recognize on the chart. (There will probably be many characters who are completely unfamiliar.) Then look for the main "action" of Bible history—the connection from Adam to Abraham to Judah to David to Jesus. Point out that history doesn't just "happen" as time goes on. In retrospect, group members should see that God has a specific plan, and each individual is part of that plan. As you examine the chart, let group members ask questions as you make relevant comments from the session.

Step 3
Instead of a traditional sword drill, conduct a Bible *character* sword drill. Make a list of several Bible characters, specific stories that involve them, and the Scripture passages where the stories are found. Explain that when you call out the name of a character and a specific story (for example, **Elijah—being taken to heaven in a whirlwind**), kids may begin searching their Bible for the passage. The first person to find the passage (in this case, II Kings 2:11) must stand and call it out. You will then quickly summarize the story and move on to the next character. Award small prizes to each winner, if possible.

URBAN

Step 3
Many of your inner city kids are probably aware that they've lived *far* from perfect lives. In fact, this realization may be keeping some of them from receiving Christ as Savior. They may view God as a "big lightning bolt in the sky," waiting to "zap" them for their sins the minute they acknowledge Him. Read Romans 3:23 to your kids to assure them that "all have sinned and fall short of the glory of God"—even the faithful Old Testament characters mentioned in Hebrews 11. Follow up that verse by reading Philippians 3:13, 14 ("Forgetting what is behind and straining toward what is ahead, I press on toward the goal to win the prize for which God has called me heavenward in Christ Jesus"). Point out that all we can do is keep our eyes on Christ, ask forgiveness for our past sins, and try to live for Him day by day.

Step 4
If you can't find a panel of adults for your kids to interview, try using the testimonies of more famous Christians. You'll need to find several videotapes, books, and/or magazine articles in which Christian athletes like Mike Singletary (formerly of the Chicago Bears), Kevin Johnson, David Robinson, and A.C. Green share what God has done in their lives. Even though your kids won't be able to ask these people questions about their testimonies, it's likely that your group members will pay close attention to what they have to say.

JR. HIGH / HIGH SCHOOL COMBINED

Step 4
As part of recognizing the *contemporary* faithful people of God, you might want to begin with a Parents Appreciation Night. Plan to set aside a future meeting time to give thanks for all that your kids' parents have done for them. (Daring groups might even want to try to cook a dinner for the parents.) Spend some time during this step clarifying what your group members would like to say and do to help parents feel more appreciated. Come up with a program (and perhaps a menu) to show parents how much they mean to your group members. Young people (especially junior highers) need to make strong efforts to stay close to their parents. This is a time of life when many parent-child relationships are tested. The more commitment the *kids* make to keeping the relationship strong, the more likely the parents will be to trust them and give them more freedom to grow. (And when you've planned your Parents Appreciation Night, a good sequel might be Pastor Appreciation Night.)

Step 5
Instruct your high schoolers to write on the back of Repro Resource 4 the top three things they think junior highers notice about their (the high schoolers') lives. Some may list things like the way they talk and the way they treat others. Others may name things like the way they dress and the kind of car they drive. Then have your junior highers write down the top three things they *actually* notice about high schoolers. When everyone is finished, collect the lists (keeping the sheets of the two age groups separate). Then read the lists aloud. This activity should demonstrate to your high schoolers that they are role models for younger kids—whether they like it or not.

EXTRA CHALLENGE

Step 2
As you're discussing the various characters in the Bible, have group members form a "common bond chain" that connects as many characters as possible. Provide one name to get things started. Let's say you begin with Adam. The first person should then think of a character who has something in common with Adam. It might be Eve, his wife. It might be Noah, who also got in trouble while naked (Genesis 9:20-27). It might be Paul, who also had an encounter with a serpent (Acts 28:3-6). Once a character's name has been used, that character may not be used again—nor may the association. (Otherwise, group members might spend a half hour exhausting all of the *males* of the Bible.) This may be difficult at first, but challenge group members to make a game of this from time to time. It's a good exercise to make connections between stories that aren't usually associated. In addition to being a means of associating different stories, it also helps group members think in broad terms of the Bible as being a whole, rather than limiting their thinking to one independent story at a time.

Step 5
Say: **Most of you probably think you know a lot about Bible characters. Here's your chance to prove it.** Write the names of several Bible characters on slips of paper and put them in a container. Have each group member draw a slip. Then instruct kids to write a half-page to one-page report on the character they picked. Encourage them to be creative in their reports, perhaps writing in first-person as the character. Throw a couple of not-so-well-known names into the mix to liven up the activity. Names like Achan and Hymenaeus may cause kids to do a double-take when they're expecting names like Adam and Moses. As you wrap up the session, remind group members to bring their reports to the next meeting so they can read them aloud to the group.

PLANNING CHECKLIST

Date Used:

Approx. Time

Step 1: The Piece That Passes Understanding ______
- o Extra Action
- o Large Group
- o Extra Fun
- o Media
- o Short Meeting Time

Step 2: Good Connections ______
- o Small Group
- o Heard It All Before
- o Little Bible Background
- o Mostly Girls
- o Mostly Guys
- o Extra Fun
- o Extra Challenge

Step 3: We're Being Watched ______
- o Heard It All Before
- o Little Bible Background
- o Fellowship & Worship
- o Mostly Girls
- o Mostly Guys
- o Short Meeting Time
- o Urban

Step 4: Contemporary Characters ______
- o Small Group
- o Fellowship & Worship
- o Media
- o Urban
- o Combined Jr. High/High School

Step 5: People of God: The Next Generation ______
- o Extra Action
- o Large Group
- o Combined Jr. High/High School
- o Extra Challenge

SESSION

3 Breaking the Code

YOUR GOALS FOR THIS SESSION:

Choose one or more

- [ ] To help kids see that the Bible isn't hard to comprehend if they seriously try to understand it.
- [ ] To help kids identify obstacles that prevent them from comprehending the Word of God, and to establish goals to get past such obstacles.
- [ ] To help kids learn to use available tools to figure out the parts of the Bible they just can't make any sense of.
- [ ] Other ______________________________

Your Bible Base:

Matthew 13:1-23

STEP 1

Tales from the Cryptogram

(Needed: Copies of Repro Resource 5, pencils)

OPTIONS

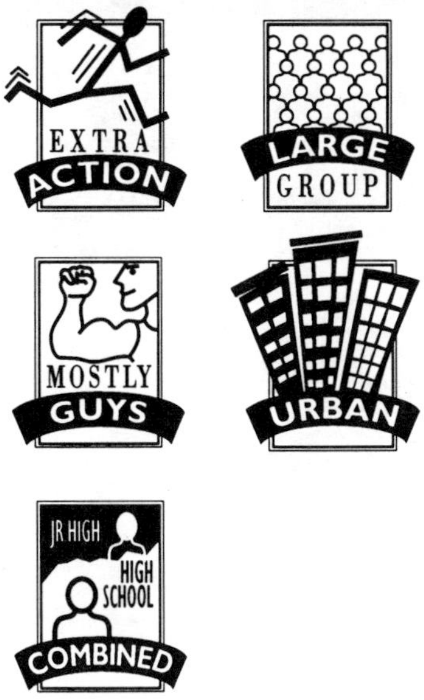

Hand out copies of "Code Dread" (Repro Resource 5) and pencils. Have group members work on the codes listed on the sheet. Some are fairly simple, but most are rather difficult. The goal is to have the kids struggle quite a bit and feel a certain sense of frustration, but not to make them feel stupid. Consequently, you might want to have them work in groups rather than individually. Also be ready to provide clues along the way (one word from the sentence, a couple of letters that have been substituted for other ones, etc.). One other clue you might want to give: The word *code* appears in every sentence.

After a while, see how many of the codes were broken by your group members. Also check to see how many of the codes were recognized by your young people. And while you will probably have no problem solving them yourself, here are the answers just in case:

1. "If you think this is Morse Code, you are absolutely right."
2. "If you read this sentence backward, you will break the code quickly."
3. "If these dots were raised, this would be a Braille code."
4. "In this code, each letter is shifted two letters down the alphabet." [A = C, B = D, etc.]
5. "These code numbers represent the positions of the letters in the alphabet." [1 = A, 2 = B, etc.]

Some of your group members might be able to figure out the Braille and Morse codes by working out the letter combinations. But explain that it certainly would have been much easier if they had the keys to each of the codes. It would then be no trouble to figure out the sentences, and frustration would have been greatly reduced. Point out that it's not that the sentences are unclear. It's simply that group members are missing something they need in order to "translate."

STEP 2

Wheel of Biblical Confusion

(Needed: Chalkboard and chalk or newsprint and marker, list of biblical words and phrases)

Ask: **Does it ever seem to you that the Bible is written in some kind of code? Explain.** Note group members' comments and try to deal with them as you go through the session. But first try to draw out some specific examples with a quick game of "Wheel of Fortune" (without the wheel). You may play with three volunteers at a time or you may divide into teams and let group members play as a team. Make a list of biblical names, places, phrases, etc. that might be obscure, difficult to understand, or otherwise challenging. Then write the category on the board and draw underlines to indicate the number of words and letters in the puzzle you have selected. Players may guess consonants until they miss. They may guess the solution at any time. But if they select a letter that isn't in the puzzle or guess the solution incorrectly, play resumes with the next person or team. Below are a few suggestions to get you started. (The terms may vary based on the Bible translation used. These are taken from the NIV translation.)

OPTIONS

People
Melchizedek (Genesis 14)
King Nebuchadnezzar (Daniel 1–4)
King Xerxes and Queen Vashti (Esther 1)
Ananias and Sapphira (Acts 5)
Bildad the Shuhite (Job 2)

Places
Canaan (Numbers 13)
Mount Nebo (Deuteronomy 32)
Armageddon (Revelation 16)
The Negev (Genesis 12)
The third heaven (II Corinthians 12)

Things
Urim and Thummim (Exodus 28)
Asherah pole (Judges 6)
Seraphs (Isaiah 6)
Eunuch (Acts 8)
Leviathan (Isaiah 27)

Words/Phrases
Day of Atonement (Leviticus 16)
Feast of Ingathering (Exodus 23)
Son of Man (Matthew 8)
Sacrifice of praise (Hebrews 13)
The abomination that causes desolation (Matthew 24)

Select words and phrases your group members have covered in the past and should know, yet may still be confused about. As each word or phrase is solved, quiz group members to see how much they know about it. Try to raise a number of questions concerning strange and unusual names and places, as well as the biblical style of writing itself. (Keep track of the questions at this point. In Step 5, you will have an opportunity to try to answer some of them.)

Explain that even when we figure out the spelling and pronunciation of such words, we still have to deal with some very unusual names, places, and objects.

Ask: **What do you do when you come across a portion of Scripture that you simply can't understand?** (Skip over the hard parts; give up trying to get *anything* out of the Bible; use reference materials to help understand; ask for help from someone who knows more; etc.)

STEP 3

Peter Pollin' Mary

OPTIONS

Sometimes it's difficult for young people to clearly express what they think about certain topics, or to put their feelings into words. To facilitate your discussion of the difficulties of reading the Bible, read a number of statements and poll your group members to see whether they agree or disagree with each one. Group members should stand if they agree and remain seated if they disagree.

You may create your own list of agree/disagree statements, but here are a few to get you started:

- **I find many parts of the Bible too difficult to understand.**
- **More people would study the Bible if it wasn't so hard to comprehend.**
- **I have trouble finding what I'm looking for in the Bible.**
- **I think regular—almost daily—Bible reading is very important.**
- **I read and study the Bible almost every day.**
- **There's too much unnecessary stuff in the Bible.**
- **The Bible would be easier to understand if the names and places weren't so weird.**

Perhaps your group members' agree/disagree responses will generate some questions or discussion. If so, deal with any issues that are raised. Encourage everyone to be honest about any difficulty or frustration he or she faces when it comes to Bible study.

Then ask: Since we place so much importance on knowing what the Bible has to say, why are so many parts of it hard for us to understand? Let kids respond with their opinions, but hold off on reaching any conclusions until after the Bible study.

STEP 4

A Seedy Story

(Needed: Bibles, copies of Repro Resource 6, pencils)

Explain: **Complaints about biblical teaching are not new. As a matter of fact, as soon as Jesus began to teach, people began to notice that they couldn't quite keep up with everything He was trying to tell them. One of the first things they discovered was that Jesus' teaching was much different than that of the religious leaders they were accustomed to hearing. It was easy to believe that Jesus knew exactly what He was talking about** (Matthew 7:28, 29)**, but even Jesus' disciples had trouble at times as they searched for the "real" meanings of the stories Jesus told.**

Have group members listen or follow along as you read Matthew 13:1-9 (the Parable of the Sower). This is such a frequently taught passage that it may no longer hold much intrigue for some of your group members. But ask them to listen as if they were hearing the story for the first time.

Afterward, ask: **Suppose you went to church, knowing little about the pastor—or about Christianity, for that matter. The pastor gets up, tells the story you just heard, and sits down again. What would you think? Would you go home spiritually enriched? If not, how do you think you would feel?** Some people might think they had stumbled into the Farm Bureau rather than the church. Some might be very confused as to the purpose of the story. Those who thought the pastor was a good and wise man might try to analyze what he had said, much as they would try to figure out a riddle. Others might ignore the story or treat it as a bunch of nonsense.

Explain: **Jesus' disciples took another approach—they waited until He got away from the crowd and then asked Him what He meant** (Matthew 13:10; Luke 8:9). **And what He told them is**

OPTIONS

LARGE GROUP

FELLOWSHIP & WORSHIP

MOSTLY GUYS

EXTRA FUN

JR. HIGH HIGH SCHOOL COMBINED

still very applicable to us today. But before we look at what He told them, let's see what *you* think the parable means.

Hand out copies of "Sower Losers" (Repro Resource 6). Have everyone fill out the sheet. Group members will be asked to examine what they think Jesus meant. They will also be challenged to come up with some specific examples as to how the things Jesus described might actually take place in their lives. Give them some time to struggle with this for a while.

If they are confused as to what they're supposed to do, give an example: **Jesus tells us that the birds represent "the evil one [who] comes and snatches away what was sown in [a person's] heart." But when this happens to a person, we don't see birds and we don't see Satan. What might we actually see in the person's life?** (Open hostility toward Christian things? A refusal to go to church at all?) **These responses are what you should put in the last column.**

When group members finish, discuss their findings. After some speculative discussion, have someone read Matthew 13:18-23 to see what Jesus actually told His disciples. See how well your kids did at coming up with Jesus' intended meaning. Use the following information to supplement your discussion of Jesus' interpretation.

According to Jesus, one of the barriers to understanding the Word of God (the Bible) is the ongoing *spiritual conflict* we face. Satan doesn't want God to communicate clearly to us. Even though we may attend church and hear God's Word on a regular basis, it may never take root. Personal examples from your group members might include any kind of temptations they face. It's always tempting to do something else rather than apply oneself to Bible study. The other activities don't even have to be "bad" in and of themselves. Any number of things (even friends and family) can "snatch away" the "seed" of God's Word and prevent it from having its intended effect.

A second barrier to understanding the Bible is the *failure to mature spiritually*. Many of your kids may know people who became Christians and seemed to be genuinely excited about it, yet who fell away from the faith after the newness of the experience wore off. Jesus explains with His agricultural parable that we need to "put down roots." We can hear God's Word, get excited about it, and let it have an effect in our lives. But until we "go a little deeper" and develop "below the surface," we won't be able to cope with the pressures of life that we face. We usually don't have to look far to find a bunch of "wilted" Christians.

A third barrier to effective Bible study is *distraction*. Few of us, upon becoming Christians, will enter a monastery or convent. We will continue to face the "real" world with "the worries of this life and the deceitfulness of wealth" (among other concerns). It's very easy to focus more on our anxieties and daily routine than it is to keep our minds set "on things above" (Colossians 3:2). We become easily distracted from the Word of God—the one thing that helps us keep all of these other things in proper perspective. We must not allow anything else to "choke" out the thing that is most important. Just as we weed a garden to ensure the best growth of the flowers or vegetables, we need to weed out any activities that prevent our spiritual growth.

Your group members should make the previous observations as well as coming up with specific ways to avoid all three barriers to understanding God's Word. Let them share the things they come up with.

Then ask: How can you tell if someone is being "successful" in his or her study of the Bible? According to Jesus, when God's Word is heard and understood, the result will be a fruitful spiritual life. Few of us can claim we never hear God's Word. (And whether or not we hear it, we still have access to the *written* Word all of the time). But it is very likely that many of us allow one of the previous obstacles to prevent us from *understanding* and *applying* it; therefore, we don't fully experience fruitful lives. We lose out on seeing what we could accomplish (with God's help), and Christianity as a whole suffers because we forfeit what we could and should be contributing to the church body.

STEP 5

Tools and Tactics

(Needed: Paper, pencils, Bible reference materials)

Say: **When people complain about the Bible's being so difficult to understand, do you think most of them have already tried as hard as possible to figure out the parts that confuse them?** Let kids respond.

Then continue: **Jesus tells us that three major reasons we fail to let the Bible speak clearly to us are (1) Satan's work to prevent our grasping God's Word, (2) our own attempts to grow without being firmly rooted, and (3) our willingness to give other concerns top priority. What percent of the time do you think one of these three causes is the *real* reason behind our inability to comprehend something the Bible has to say?**

While these three obstacles may not account for *every* instance of biblical confusion, we need to be aware of them and make a mental note to check for them occasionally. Whenever we find that we're not getting as much as we feel we should out of Bible study, we need to

OPTIONS

examine our lives to see if one of these negative influences has crept in. However, there is one other important principle to explain why some parts of the Bible are so much harder to understand than others.

Ask: **Could God have provided us with a Bible in a language at, say, a third-grade level? If so, why didn't He?** (While some of the theological aspects of Scripture are a bit complicated, it seems that much of the content could be a lot easier to understand.)

Why are parts of the Bible so symbolic? For example, why did Jesus use parables? Why not just come right out and say what He meant? Let kids respond.

Explain: **In between the telling of the Parable of the Sower, and His explanation of it, Jesus explains why He used parables. And in doing so, He reveals a very important principle we need to keep in mind. Listen carefully to His comments.**

Have someone read Matthew 13:10-17. Then discuss the following questions. Suggested answers are provided, but before you provide answers, first allow group members to struggle to discover them. Allow kids to feel a bit uncertain as you lead them into the activity that follows.

Why did Jesus use parables in His teaching? (Parables are a kind of "code." They hide a deeper meaning. Jesus used them so His followers would keep thinking about what He was saying until they "figured it out.")

Is Jesus trying to keep some people "in the dark" about God and His kingdom? (God desires for everyone to turn to Him [II Peter 3:9]. Yet He knows that some people are hard-hearted and don't really care about what He has to tell them.)

What do you think verse 12 means: "Whoever has will be given more, and he will have an abundance. Whoever does not have, even what he has will be taken from him"? Sometimes people apply this verse out of context, and it sounds terribly unfair. Yet in the context of better understanding Jesus' teachings, He suggests that those who continue to use biblical knowledge will keep adding to their understanding. Those who make no effort to do so will be unable to make sense of what little they do know.

What does the rest of this passage mean—all of the stuff about "ever hearing but never understanding" and "prophets . . . longed to see what you see but did not see it"?

Keep asking hard questions until several of your group members seem somewhat confused or overwhelmed. Then say: **This is an instance of not understanding something the Bible has to say. So what can we do about it?**

Have on hand several Bible reference resources. Briefly demonstrate how each one might be used in this case. If you wish, you can divide into groups and let each group take one of the resources to better understand Matthew 13:10-17. For example:

• Dictionary—Some people may need definitions of *calloused* (vs. 15), *righteous* (vs. 17), and so forth.

• Bible dictionary—Check for the significance of parables, the meaning of "the kingdom of heaven" (vs. 11), a short biography of Isaiah (vs. 14), and so forth.

• Commentaries—See what wisdom several Bible scholars can shed on this particular passage.

• Concordance—Look up other references to *kingdom of heaven*, *seeing*, *hearing*, and so forth.

• Cross references—Find the original sources of the passages Jesus is quoting, and see what else can be discovered through references to other verses.

By the time you use most of these resources, your group's understanding of what Jesus was saying should be greatly increased. If time permits, use the references to look up some of the "Wheel of Fortune" words and phrases that seemed to confuse group members. If not, have them do so as an assignment for the next meeting.

Close with a challenge for your group members not to be so quick to give up when they find hard-to-understand passages or verses that make no sense to them. With a better knowledge of how to use Bible reference resources, and the availability of yourself and other leaders as *human* resources, your kids should soon "produce a crop [yielding] a hundred, sixty or thirty times what was sown."

Code Dread

Are you one of those people who enjoys a good puzzle? Or do you prefer to have things spelled out for you? Either way, here's an activity you should enjoy. As you can see, everything is spelled out. The trouble is, it's spelled in the wrong letters or other symbols. See how many of the following codes you can break. Some of them are pretty hard, but if you're extra nice (or willing to lay out a bribe) your group leader might provide you with some clues if you get stumped.

1. •• ••–•/–•–– ––– ••–/– •••• •• –• –•–/– •••• •• •••/
•• •••/–– ––– •–• ••• •/–•–• ––– –•• •/–•–– ––– ••–/
•– •–• •/•– –••• ••• ––– •–•• ••– – • •–•• –•––/
•–• •• ––• •••• –

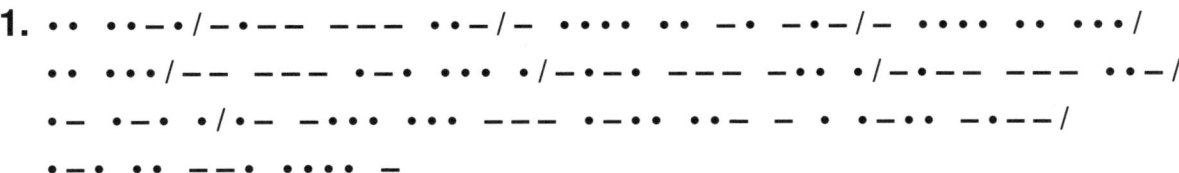

2. YLK CIU QEDO CEHTKA ERBLLI WUO YDRA WK CABE CNET

NESSIH TD AERU OYFI.

3. 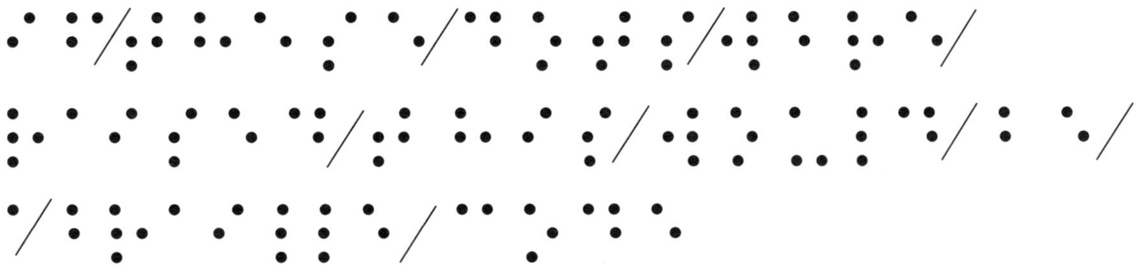

4. KP VJKU EQFG, GCEJ NGVVGT KU UJKHVGF VYQ NGVVGTU FQYP

VJG CNRJCDGV.

5. 20-8-5-19-5 3-15-4-5 14-21-13-2-5-18-19 18-5-16-18-5-19-5-14-20 20-8-5

16-15-19-9-20-9-15-14-19 15-6 20-8-5 12-5-20-20-5-18-19 9-14 20-8-5

1-12-16-8-1-2-5-20.

SOWER LOSERS

When Jesus told the Parable of the Sower (Matthew 13:1-23), He confused a lot of people—including His own disciples. Because He used symbolic images, He left a lot of people scratching their heads and wondering if they should go home and plant something. But that's not what He meant at all.

What do *you* get out of His parable? For each of the following things He describes, explain what you think He is talking about. Then after you give a general description of each problem area, get more specific about each particular problem. For example, Jesus finally explained the parable to His disciples (vss. 18-23), so you can put His "general" explanation in the first column. But even though Jesus explained *what* His symbolism meant, He didn't tell us exactly *how* those things might actually take place in our lives. That's up to you. Your specific examples should go in the second column.

Problem	In general, what do you think Jesus meant?	How might these things take place in your life?
 "Some [seed] fell along the path, and the birds came and ate it up."		
 "Some fell on rocky places, where it did not have much soil. It sprang up quickly. . . . But when the sun came up, the plants were scorched, and they withered because they had no root."		
 "Other seed fell among thorns, which grew up and choked the plants."		

EXTRA ACTION

Step 1
Have group members form pairs. As an alternative to Repro Resource 5, or in addition to it, provide the pairs with keys to Morse Code, Braille, or other codes. (These keys can be found in most encyclopedias.) Or you might give the pairs foreign language dictionaries. Then have the members of each pair attempt to send messages back and forth, with the first person asking a question and the second person answering it. Kids will quickly discover that even with the keys in front of them, it takes practice to get used to sending and receiving messages in these various codes or foreign languages. With time and practice it becomes natural and automatic; but at first, it takes some getting used to. The same may be true of Bible study.

Step 3
Rather than having them simply stand or sit to show agreement/disagreement with the opinion statements, designate the individuals in your group as human "Jog-O-Meters." Explain that the more they agree with a statement, the faster they should run in place. Then go through each of the statements. (You may want to rephrase some of them to get more variety in the pace of your group members' activity.) Group members will probably be too busy laughing and panting to give serious thought to the statements as you are reading them; so when you're finished, be sure to review what the common opinion seemed to be for each statement. Discuss any differences of opinion at that point.

SMALL GROUP

Step 3
With a small group, you might want to replace the opinion poll with a roleplay that will accomplish the same purpose. Assign one of your group members the role of a person who is convinced that the Bible is a holy book, but that it's just too hard for "normal" people to understand. He or she has simply given up trying. The other group members should all try to convince the person of the merits of Bible reading. This roleplay should bring out many of the arguments that people give for not reading the Bible (as well as arguments *for* reading it). But in a roleplay, an honest actor may come up with some legitimate reasons that defy "the usual" reasons for Bible reading. If we're honest, we must admit that even many adults shy away from large portions of Scripture because of its difficulty or because of their own lack of knowledge of the historical context. Encourage group members to be completely open about any such feelings they have. Only then will you be able to help them deal with those feelings.

Step 5
When you discuss tools and resources that can help your kids understand Scripture, emphasize that one good resource is other knowledgeable people. Reference materials may be readily available, yet most people tend to turn to friends for help and advice. It's much easier (and more fun) to ask someone about something we don't understand than to conduct a "research project" to find out what we want to know. However, in small groups, *human* resources may be scarce. If possible, you might want to have your youth group meet with another group (college/career, young adults, adults, or whatever). Host an informal get-together to let your group members meet and mingle with other people in your church, and to get to know them better. Help your kids see that there are additional sources of advice (and human contact) available to them beyond the small number of people in the group.

LARGE GROUP

Step 1
Prior to the meeting, gather several locks and keys (or combinations). To begin the session, give half your group members locks and the other half keys (or combinations). Have everyone try to find his or her partner. Use this exercise to point out that we may need to accumulate more than one "key" to "unlock" Scripture. Reading the Bible is certainly a good starting point. But some portions of the Bible may defy our understanding if all we do is give them a cursory read-through. We may need other "keys": prayer for wisdom, reference materials, advice from other people, Bible memorization, and so forth.

Step 4
Have your kids form three groups. Instruct the members of each group to work together to complete Repro Resource 6. When everyone is finished, assign one "Problem" on the sheet to each group. Instruct the members of each group to create a skit that will demonstrate some of the specific applications they came up with for their assigned "Problem." (For example, it's one thing to know that the birds that ate the seed represent "the evil one [who] comes and snatches away what was sown in [one's] heart." But the group's skit should indicate some *specific* ways that this could happen in a person's life.) After the groups have performed their skits, discuss any questions group members have about the parable.

OPTIONS

SESSION THREE

Step 2
Play "Super Advanced Bible Picture Charades for Geniuses." Essentially, this is a version of Pictionary™, using the words, objects, and concepts provided in Step 2 of the session. Teams will compete to see which one can guess first what one of its members is drawing. Using such difficult words will probably be very frustrating for contestants. Perhaps your "heard it all before" group is good at *recognizing* Bible words, names, and places. But often it is quite another thing to *understand* those terms well enough to draw them so someone else can recognize them. Explain that similar distinctions can be made between hearing God's Word and applying it. Just because we hear something doesn't mean we automatically put it into practice.

Step 3
Conduct a Christmas carol quiz. Read a line from a carol and ask kids to write down which carol the line comes from. Select lines that contain words or phrases that are somewhat difficult to understand. Here are a few to get you started:

• "He comes to make his blessing flow far as the curse is found" ("Joy to the World")
• "For lo, the days are hast'ning on, By prophets seen of old, When with the evercircling years shall come the time foretold" ("It Came upon the Midnight Clear")
• "Veiled in flesh, the Godhead see; hail th' incarnate Deity; pleased as man with men to dwell, Jesus our Emmanuel" ("Hark! The Herald Angels Sing")
• "Word of the Father, now in flesh appearing" ("O Come, All Ye Faithful")

When you finish the quiz, discuss exactly what these lines mean. If you can stump some of your kids on a few of the carols and their messages, point out that the same principle holds true about the Bible. Sometimes we hear stories or sermons about certain passages so many times that we think we know them pretty well. Yet in reality we may be hearing without comprehending.

Step 2
Prior to the meeting, find a contract, a professional journal, or some other resource that contains a lot of difficult-to-understand language. Or if you feel especially creative, use a dictionary and thesaurus to write a few cerebral, erudite, sagacious paragraphs of your own. Let group members struggle to understand the message that is being conveyed in the text. If they need to, let them use a dictionary to help them figure out some of the hard words. (And, by the way, there should be no eructation during this activity.) Point out that we must learn to tolerate a certain amount of difficult reading material. It's part of life. We can't avoid it, no matter how hard we try. Consequently, we shouldn't try to skip the parts of the Bible that are a little difficult to understand. Just as people aren't likely to buy a house without struggling through the "legalese" language on the contract, your group members shouldn't try to get through adolescence without starting to struggle a bit to better understand more of the Bible. Encourage them to start with what they *do* understand and move on from there.

Step 5
If your group members don't know the Bible very well, they aren't likely to know what their options are when it comes to Bible study. Provide a variety of Bible translations and paraphrases for them to examine: *King James Version, New King James Version, New International Version, New American Standard Bible, The Living Bible, Phillips Translation*, etc. If possible, give each person a different version to examine. Choose some short passages to read from each of the versions (such as Psalm 23; Luke 2:1-7; etc.). Help group members see that understanding the Bible might begin with finding a translation that makes sense to them.

Step 4
Depending on the season, try to bring in some wildflowers, dandelions, thistle blooms, or other kind of "pretty weeds." (If it's the middle of winter, you'll have to use your imagination.) Point out the beauty of the plants. They may be colorful, sweet-smelling, edible, or have any number of other positive characteristics. Yet if they are allowed to grow in a yard or garden, they will choke out healthy plants. And if they aren't dealt with one year, they will come back stronger the next. Use this illustration with the Parable of the Sower to point out that not all of the "thorns" in our life are easily recognized as weeds. We may have some beautiful, seemingly sweet, lovely people or habits that take our time and prevent us from growing spiritually. Challenge group members to examine their lives—relationships, use of time, habits, and so forth—to determine whether or not they may have some "pretty weeds" springing up. They may not be sure about certain things, which is fine. The important thing is that they begin to question and examine such things to ensure their continued growth. Later, close the session by praising God for the spiritual lessons He provides through nature. Ask for His wisdom in "weeding out" influences that get in the way of a better relationship with Him.

Step 5
While it is important to try to understand as much as we can about the Bible, you might want to close by giving thanks to God that He doesn't judge any of us based on IQ or vocabulary skills. Offer praise that the most important parts of Scripture are clear and simple. Point out that as we respond to the plain truth that requires only childlike understanding and faith, God will eventually provide the wisdom we need to move ahead from there. And while we should certainly work toward knowing and comprehending whatever we can, we shouldn't feel bad or incompetent as we continue to learn.

MOSTLY GIRLS

Step 3

Add the following agree/disagree statements to your list:

• **I'd get more out of the Bible if more women were included in it.**
• **The Bible has become outdated, especially in regard to women's rights and roles.**
• **Paraphrases of the Bible are very helpful and needed; they make it more relevant to today.**

If you have time, ask your girls to write their own agree/disagree statements on a piece of paper. After a few minutes, collect the sheets; allow the group to respond as you read the statements anonymously. (This activity may give you even further insight as to some of the frustrations your group members have about the Bible.)

Step 5

On a large piece of newsprint or chalkboard, draw three columns. At the top of the first column, write "Satan"; at the top of the second column, write "No Roots"; at the top of the third column, write "Other Priorities." Have your girls name as many specific examples as possible for each column. Afterward, talk about the *specific* areas that are a struggle for your girls. For example, if some girls have a tendency to spend time on "Other Priorities"—such as over-involvement at school—brainstorm specific steps they can take to help alleviate that problem.

MOSTLY GUYS

Step 1

Have your guys roleplay asking a girl out on a date. Set the scene so that several guys are trying to impress the same girl and convince her to go out. They should use their best lines on her and describe the kind of date they have in mind. The guys shouldn't be aware of it, but the girl (or the person roleplaying the girl) should be given a "key to her heart"—something she likes doing better than anything else. It might be eating out, horseback riding, shopping, sports, or whatever. If a guy happens to mention whatever it is she really enjoys, she should accept his offer. Otherwise, she should decline. If time permits, do a couple of similar roleplays, changing the "key" each time. If your guys are a little thick-headed when it comes to seeing the importance of finding keys to more effective Bible study, they may be able to relate to this object lesson.

Step 4

Point out that Jesus' disciples were, for the most part, a pretty average group of guys. We tend to think that they were pretty holy and spiritual. Yet when we look closely at the Parable of the Sower, we see them pull Jesus aside and ask, "What are you *talking* about?!" Most guys ought to relate to that feeling. So ask: **What have you come across in the Bible lately that you just don't understand? If you could pull Jesus aside for a little one-on-one conversation, without any outside distractions, what would you want Him to explain to you?** After group members respond, explain that the whole purpose of Bible study and prayer is to "pull Jesus aside" and allow Him to communicate with us. It may take a bit of perseverance and effort before we finally begin to understand, but if we don't give up, usually we can start to make sense of the things that confuse us.

EXTRA FUN

Step 4

Bring in a watermelon or pumpkin. Have kids form two teams. Cut the watermelon or pumpkin into halves. Have a contest to see which team can get the most seeds out of its half in two minutes. The catch is that group members may use only *spoons* to get the seeds out—no hands or anything else. After two minutes, have both teams count their seeds. Award prizes to the team with the most seeds. Use the topic of seeds to lead in to a discussion on the parable of the sower.

Step 5

All of the discussion in this step about using tools can sound mechanical and boring. So to show group members that tools can be our friends, conclude with a party of some kind in which all of the elements are provided except the "tools." You might have ice cream (without spoons or scoops), cans of syrup (without can openers), nuts (without nutcrackers), and so forth. The kind of food you plan will determine your need for tools. Be creative. But whatever you plan, you can begin without bowls or utensils. Then point out that just as spoons and bowls can vastly intensify the enjoyment of a hot fudge sundae, so can the appropriate reference materials enhance what we can learn from a difficult passage of Scripture.

MEDIA

Step 3
After you address group members' opinions about the Bible, ask: **What can we do to better understand the difficult portions of the Bible?** Then, before kids respond, say: **Better yet, I wonder how cable television would handle the issue of making the Bible easier to understand.** Pretend to click through the channels of cable television with the assumption that each program will be devoted to explaining hard parts of Scripture. Ask: **What might the following channels do to help viewers understand and appreciate portions of the Bible that might otherwise go unread?** The channels are as follows: The Discovery Channel (which focuses on science and nature), Arts and Entertainment, The Disney Channel, ESPN, CNN, M-TV, Nickelodeon (the children's network), Comedy Central, and The Nashville Network. While kids may not come up with much for *all* of these channels, some of the "networks" should provide fairly original approaches to the Bible. Challenge your group members to deal with Scripture at various levels as they read and reread some of the more difficult portions.

Step 5
Wrap up the session by showing a symbolic Christian film or video. Choose one that contains clear symbolism that group members should have no problem understanding (perhaps a version of *The Lion, the Witch, and the Wardrobe*). Your kids should see that symbolism can not only be easy to understand, but may even be a *better* method of getting a point across than a straightforward presentation of facts. When your group members come across biblical symbolism, encourage them not to automatically resist it. Explain that perhaps the symbolism will help them understand God's truth better than they could without it.

SHORT MEETING TIME

Step 2
Begin the session with the "Wheel of Fortune" activity in Step 2, as if it were a normal game and without any warning that the answers are very difficult. After two or three rounds, listen for any grumblings or complaints. When you begin to hear them, challenge group members to get more involved in the portions of the Bible that may seem difficult to them. Read or summarize Jesus' Parable of the Sower (Step 4) to demonstrate the importance of allowing God's Word to take root in our lives. Then spend most of your time in Step 5, discussing the intent of parables and symbolic writing, and learning how to use the right tools to better understand those portions of Scripture.

Step 3
To make the most of the time you have, let kids come up with their own reasons for why the Bible is difficult for them to get into on a regular basis. Give kids a few minutes to come up with their reasons. Then ask for a few volunteers to pantomime some of the reasons they came up with. As each volunteer "performs," let the rest of the group try to guess what his or her reason is. For example, one person might lay down on the floor and pretend to be asleep to illustrate being too tired to read the Bible. After a few group members have performed, ask others to call out the reasons they came up with.

URBAN

Step 1
Add the following code to Repro Resource 5:

- **Or-fay od-gay o-say oved-lay ee-thay orld-way at-thay ee-hay ave-gay is-hay ee-onlay egotten-bay on-say at-thay oever-whay elieves-bay en-iay im-hay all-shay ot-nay erish-pay ut-bay ave-hay erlasting-evhay ife-lay.** (This is a Pig Latin code for the text of John 3:16.)

Step 5
While discussing the three major reasons we fail to let the Bible speak clearly to us, it may be helpful to have your teens review Matthew 4:1-11 (Jesus' temptation in the wilderness). Discuss as a group the tactics Satan used to try to keep Jesus from focusing on His mission and the tools Jesus used to thwart Satan's plan. Then come up with an "urban equivalent" for each tactic in the story. For example, an urban equivalent of Satan's offer of all of the kingdoms in the world might be someone offering a young urban teen drugs or illicit sex. In essence, this is an appeal to a "You can have it all" mindset. Help your kids recognize what Jesus knew: the most powerful weapon against such temptations is God's Word.

JR. HIGH HIGH SCHOOL COMBINED

EXTRA CHALLENGE

PLANNING CHECKLIST

Step 1
Begin the session with the code activity on Repro Resource 5. But before you do, secretly provide your junior highers with keys to most of the codes. (The keys to Morse Code and Braille can be found in most encyclopedias. You can photocopy a key for each of your junior highers as well as letting them in on the other code secrets.) Junior highers shouldn't let high schoolers know they have the keys. When you see that most of the junior highers have worked out their codes, ask: **How many of the codes have you figured out so far?** See how your high schoolers react when the junior high kids turn out to be a lot smarter than they would ever have expected. Eventually let everyone in on the secret. Then summarize: **If you devote yourselves to regular Bible study, you will eventually figure out the "keys" to the parts of the Bible that make no sense to you now. And all of you—high schoolers as well as junior highers—can be a lot more intelligent about spiritual truths than a lot of adults you know. If you don't believe me, try it and see for yourselves.**

Step 4
Before you study the Parable of the Sower, read or tell some of Aesop's Fables. After each one, ask: **What do you think is the moral to this story? How can you tell? How do you know that these aren't just a bunch of stories about wacky animals that relate to each other in strange ways?** Help group members—younger ones, especially—see the value of using symbolism to make an important point. Then move on to the Parable of the Sower, an example of a similar method of teaching, yet one that is a bit more difficult to understand. But since you've already established the value of the teaching style, the difference in the level of difficulty shouldn't seem to be such a major obstacle.

Step 3
If your group members confess to having some questions about why parts of the Bible are so confusing, point out that perhaps younger kids do too. Encourage your group members to be completely honest about their feelings when it comes to the symbolic and hard-to-understand portions of the Bible. Then, as they begin to deal with their own feelings, challenge them to think of ways that they can help make the Bible more exciting to younger kids in the church. If they're ambitious enough, your group members might want to plan a "Fun-with-the-Bible Night." Not only would younger kids enjoy the opportunity to "rub shoulders" with your group of young people, but your own group members are likely to learn more from planning and teaching the younger ones for an hour than they would in a dozen regular sessions they sit through. Be creative and come up with a plan to fit your specific kids and church.

Step 5
After kids have had an opportunity to "test drive" a variety of Bible study resources, challenge each person to become an "expert" with one of them. For instance, someone might agree to take home the Bible dictionary and get familiar with it. Someone else might spend a lot of time learning to do cross referencing. Various commentaries can be sent home with several different people, and so forth. Explain that if everyone would learn to operate one type of resource, he or she would vastly increase his or her worth as a resource *to other group members*. The next time someone has a problem and can't remember or find a passage he or she has heard that would apply to it, he or she can ask the concordance "expert." When someone comes across a strange word during personal Bible study, he or she can go to the Bible dictionary person. By working together, your kids may be able to help out with each others' problems.

Date Used:

Approx. Time

Step 1: Tales from the Cryptogram ______
o Extra Action
o Large Group
o Mostly Guys
o Urban
o Combined Jr. High/High School

Step 2: Wheel of Biblical Confusion ______
o Heard It All Before
o Little Bible Background
o Short Meeting Time

Step 3: Peter Pollin' Mary ______
o Extra Action
o Small Group
o Heard It All Before
o Mostly Girls
o Media
o Short Meeting Time
o Extra Challenge

Step 4: A Seedy Story ______
o Large Group
o Fellowship & Worship
o Mostly Guys
o Extra Fun
o Combined Jr. High/High School

Step 5: Tools and Tactics ______
o Small Group
o Little Bible Background
o Fellowship & Worship
o Mostly Girls
o Extra Fun
o Media
o Urban
o Extra Challenge

SESSION 4

How'd That Get in the Bible?

YOUR GOALS FOR THIS SESSION:

Choose one or more

- [ ] To help kids recognize that the Bible contains a lot of good stories they might be missing out on, and to help them explore some of the sections they aren't quite so familiar with.
- [ ] To help kids brainstorm some reasons to be more thorough in their Bible study.
- [ ] To help kids create a list of ways to be more creative when it comes to Bible study.
- [ ] Other ______________________________

Your Bible Base:

Acts 17:1-12

Various passages that deal with the importance of knowing God's Word

STEP 1

The Match Game

(Needed: Index cards, markers)

OPTIONS

Give everyone a marker and several index cards. Explain that you will read a number of questions. After each one, group members should quickly write their answers (large enough to be seen at a distance), but not say aloud what they are writing. At your signal, they should then try to find everyone else who wrote the same answer. You might want to have group members imitate the action in the trading pit of a commodities brokerage—holding up their cards as they shout their response at the top of their lungs, seeking other people who are screaming the same thing over the roar of the crowd. If this isn't conducive to your setting, the same activity can be done in absolute silence as group members simply hold up their cards and *visually* search for matches.

Your questions should all have to do with Bible study, and should be phrased so that several answers are possible. For example:

- **What one word would you use to describe the Bible?**
- **Without repeating any word previously used, what *other* word would you use to describe the Bible?**
- **What is your favorite book of the Bible?**
- **What Old Testament book do you know the least about?**
- **What New Testament book do you know the least about?**
- **What percentage of the Bible would you say you're pretty familiar with?**
- **In your opinion, what is the most unusual Bible story?**
- **Who is a Bible character that everyone seems to know about except you?**

Though this may turn into a competition to see which group forms first, it is more important to see which are the more common responses. You should also try to see to what extent your group members are aware of the more "obscure" portions of the Bible. Do any names crop up that aren't "key players" of biblical history? Do a lot of your group members' answers tend to be the same? Do group members' responses reflect a group mentality, or does it seem that kids are reading the Bible on their own and coming across a variety of names and stories that aren't usually covered in group settings?

STEP
2

The Second String

(Needed: Copies of Repro Resource 7, pencils)

Explain: **If we grow up in a church, most of us hear about the "famous" people of the Bible. Our parents and Sunday school teachers tell us about Abraham, Noah, Moses, Samson, and so forth. They want us to read about them and imitate their faith. But in those second and third grade Sunday school classes they don't tell us that Abraham twice allowed a foreign king to think Sarah was his sister instead of his wife—even to the point of having the guy "date" his wife—just so *his* life wouldn't be in jeopardy. They don't tell us that after Noah landed the ark, he got drunk and naked. We can hardly name any of the other dozen or so judges of Israel, because Samson is the most famous one and has a really cool story to tell.**

That's the problem with "hearing" all of these good Bible stories. Until we get more involved and actually start *reading* the stories for ourselves, we miss out on a lot of the good parts. We also fail to learn about many of the other characters who may be just as important, yet aren't quite as familiar.

Hand out copies of "Who, What, and Where?" (Repro Resource 7) and pencils. Group members will get to see how much they know about some of the "second string" characters of the Bible. Without consulting their Bibles, have them try to match the character, event, and reference. After a few minutes, have each person look up one or two of the references, find the account of the character and the event, and reveal the correct matches.

The correct answers are as follows: A—17, DD; B—16, FF; C—1, EE; D—18, SS; E—4, CC; F—2, KK; G—3, TT; H—9, PP; I—20, MM; J—11, RR; K—7, LL; L—14, NN; M—5, HH; N—15, OO; O—12, JJ; P—10, QQ; Q—8, GG; R—19, BB; S—6, AA; T—13, II.

Afterward, ask: **Did anyone get all of the matches correct without having to consult the Bible—and without guessing at any of them?**

Were there any characters on the sheet that you knew absolutely nothing about? If so, which ones?

Did any of these stories sound interesting enough to check

OPTIONS

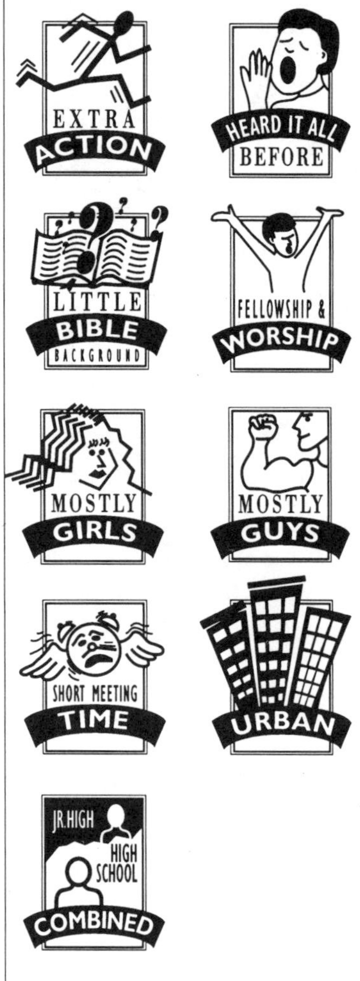

out a little more closely?

Why do you think you didn't already know all of these stories? Whose fault is it?

How do you think it will feel to get to heaven someday and meet some of these "minor" characters who did all of these incredible things, only to say, "Sorry, never heard of you"?

STEP 3

Books and Crannies

(Needed: Bibles)

OPTIONS

SMALL GROUP
FELLOWSHIP & WORSHIP
MOSTLY GIRLS
URBAN
EXTRA CHALLENGE

If group members don't know a lot of the stories listed on Repro Resource 7, they may confess that it's because they aren't particularly faithful about having personal Bible study. If so, one of the reasons may be that the Bible seems foreign to many of them. Perhaps they don't know what the Bible has to offer them, or maybe they simply can't seem to find much of interest as they leaf through its pages and stumble upon the books of law or the Minor Prophets.

To help kids discover some of the things they might find in the Bible if they look a little closer—especially in regard to some of the lesser-known stories and characters they've overlooked—conduct a sword drill that will serve as the Bible study for this session. But be aware that if kids aren't comfortable with the Bible to begin with, they are likely to feel frustrated when they start to try to find their way around the sixty-six books and hundreds of pages. So rather than having a fiercely competitive individual sword drill, have a team competition instead. Have kids form teams that combine newcomers to the Bible with those who are familiar with it. Make sure everyone has a Bible. Then give a reference and see which team can have *all* of its members find the reference first. (When the fastest people find the verses themselves, they can help other team members.) Someone from the winning team should read the verse(s) aloud.

While competition can make the Bible study a bit more fun and exciting for some groups, keep things very loose. Don't keep score or fawn over the one or two group members who always seem to find the reference first. No one should feel bad about being slow to find a passage. Before you start, explain that many of these verses are in hard-to-find books, and that the goal is to not to see who *already* knows where they are, but to let *everyone* practice finding them. As soon as you give a reference, you can also give clues to help everyone find it (explaining where short books are located in regard to larger ones, etc.)

Point out that every verse kids look up has something to do with the importance of Bible study in general or, more specifically, the need to learn more about the "tucked away" stories in the Bible. Members of the team who read the passage aloud should also explain what they think it means.

The following are some verses you may want to use. Feel free to add your own favorite passages. These have been chosen primarily to provide an assortment of Bible books to make the sword drill more challenging. They are presented in the order they will be found in the Bible, so you'll probably want to mix them up as you conduct the sword drill.

- Deuteronomy 4:1, 2—We aren't to add or take away from God's Word. (Also see Revelation 22:18, 19.) If we don't learn about *all* of the characters of the Bible, it's like "subtracting from" God's Word.
- Nehemiah 8:9, 10—While God's Word shows clearly our sinful natures and the consequences of sin, it should also be a source of great joy as we see God's provision for us.
- Hosea 14:9—We receive wisdom by understanding and applying the Word of God. We should be able to learn something about every story we read—not just the "big" ones.
- Joel 2:13—If we've strayed away from God, we shouldn't be fearful or hesitant about returning to Him. It doesn't matter how bad we are at Bible study *now* as long as we're willing to try to improve.
- Amos 3:7—We discover God's plan for us through the recorded and inspired writings of His people.
- Jonah 3:1, 2—God doesn't give up on us, even when we make mistakes. (Jonah is a classic story of how God gives us second chances.)
- Micah 6:8—God's Word shows us His expectations for us. Many times such things are shown through character studies.
- Matthew 24:35—We can count on God's Word because it is eternal.
- John 13:13-15—Through Bible study we see the example set by Jesus (and others). We need to study the lives of these people thoroughly to see how we should live.
- John 15:7, 8—When we live according to God's Word, God is glorified as He provides for our needs.
- I Timothy 4:12—In addition to *following* good examples, we should learn to *model* positive examples for others.

End the sword drill with Acts 17:10, 11. Point out how the Bereans were commended for their willingness to "[examine] the Scriptures every day" as they tried to discover God's truth.

Ask: **Do you read the Bible every day? If not, what keeps you from it? When you read the Bible, do you *examine* it to see what it has to say? Or do you just put in your five minutes or so?**

STEP 4

Too Much of a Good Thing?

(Needed: Chalkboard and chalk or newsprint and marker, suggestion box, paper, pencils, tabloid newspapers, completed copies of Repro Resource 7)

OPTIONS

LARGE GROUP

MOSTLY GUYS

MEDIA

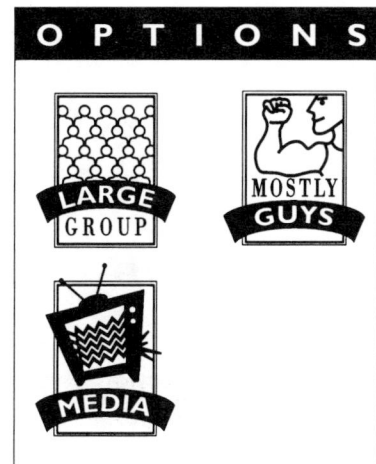

Ask: **Since there are so many verses scattered throughout the Bible that emphasize the importance of knowing God's Word, why do you think we remain unaware of so much of what's in Scripture?** Even though you may have dealt with this issue in previous sessions—and earlier in this session—let kids respond truthfully. Several of their reasons may be quite valid. (There's a *lot* of information to read and remember; we tend to know certain parts well and keep going back to them; etc.) List all of the reasons on the board as they are mentioned and number each one.

Then place a box in the center of the room. Distribute paper and pencils. Say: **This is a suggestion box. Think about the problems we've listed and what we might be able to do to remedy any or all of these problems. Write your suggestions on these slips of paper and put them in the suggestion box. You need not sign your name, but your ideas will be read aloud—so put some thought into your responses.**

Ask group members to respond by number to save time. If they want to respond to the problems numbered 2, 3, and 6, they need only write each number and their suggestion(s) for how to deal with it. After group members have placed their ideas into the suggestion box, open it and see what they came up with. You might want to deal with the number one problem first by reading and discussing all of the applicable suggestions. Then move on to number two, and so forth.

If no one mentions it, ask: **Could one of the major reasons we stop searching the Scriptures closely be that we've ceased to be amazed at God's love and power? The Bible is full of stories that detail wonderful events and incredible miracles. Yet we read the Bible with about as much enthusiasm as we do our geometry textbooks.**

Hold up a few supermarket tabloids. Note the sensationalistic headlines and the excitement the editors try to generate over ludicrous claims—the latest sighting of Elvis, another UFO invasion, or whatever.

Then ask: **What do you think might have happened if some of these writers had been around to cover the Bible stories we've been discussing?** In response, have group members form teams to report on any Bible story they wish—in the style of a supermarket tabloid. If they can think of nothing right away, they may consult their completed copies of Repro Resource 7 for some ideas and ready references. Each team should come up with at least a headline and a lead sentence. Challenge the teams to try to capture all of the thrill of the story without stretching the truth. Their stories should demonstrate that if we don't make a point of finding and reading the lesser-known stories of the Bible and giving them our close attention, we can miss out on a lot of remarkable events that have been recorded for us.

STEP 5

Taking the Study Out of Bible Study

(Needed: Copies of Repro Resource 8, pencils)

Having just demonstrated one creative method of studying the Bible, challenge group members to think of other new and better ways to interact with Scripture as a whole rather than focusing on one story at a time. Use their ideas in future sessions.

One other option is a brainstorming comparison session. For example, you might ask: **What do you think is the wettest story in the Bible?** Let kids debate whether it was Noah and the flood, Jonah, Paul's shipwreck, or some other story. Then ask: **What do you think is the *smelliest* story?** Noah and Jonah might still be contenders, in addition to Daniel in the lions' den, the Prodigal Son feeding hogs, and so forth. You can also ask about the most violent story, the most miraculous story, the best story about a woman, the best story involving a child, and so forth. In each case, list all responses given by group members and then have kids rate the stories—perhaps forming a "Top Ten" list for each category.

Hand out copies of "NO MR E" (Repro Resource 8). Let kids try to figure out each Bible character based on his or her personalized license plate. Then let them create some of their own for other Bible characters. In some cases, kids may be able to justify more than one answer for the license plate characters, but here are the intended "drivers":

1. Nicodemus (John 3:1-21)
2. Goliath (I Samuel 17:49)
3. Deborah (Judges 4)
4. Peter (Matthew 14:22-33)
5. Ruth (Ruth 2–4)

OPTIONS

6. Noah (Genesis 6–9)
7. Solomon (I Kings 4:29-34)
8. David (I Samuel 17:50)
9. Jonah (Jonah 1–2)
10. Absalom (II Samuel 18:9-15)
11. Zacchaeus (Luke 19:1-10)
12. Lazarus (John 11:38-44)
13. Methuselah (Genesis 5:27)

Challenge kids to think of new and different ways to make Bible stories come alive on a regular basis. If *they* invent games or exercises, there will probably be more interest on their part. You may need to get them started, but usually kids can come up with some very creative ideas.

Close by thanking God for the vast variety of characters described in the Bible. And ask Him for a deeper sense of determination as your group members strive to get more involved with the *whole* Bible.

WHO, WHAT, and Where?

So you think you know the Bible? We'll see. In the columns below, try to match each person with the correct event *and* the place in the Bible you'd find the story. Don't use your Bible at first. See how much you know without it. If you get stuck, ask your group leader for permission to "cheat" by looking up the references in the Bible.

	Person	*Event*	*Biblical Reference*
___ ___	A. Aaron	1. Had an unsettling conversation with his talking donkey	AA. Genesis 19:30-38
___ ___	B. Achan	2. A dead man was thrown in this person's grave and came back to life after touching the bones there	BB. Genesis 29:16-30
___ ___	C. Balaam	3. Fell asleep during a sermon and tumbled out of a third story window	CC. Genesis 34
___ ___	D. Barnabas	4. After she was raped, her brothers plotted an elaborate revenge	DD. Numbers 17
___ ___	E. Dinah	5. Hammered an opposing general's head to the ground	EE. Numbers 22:21-35
___ ___	F. Elisha	6. His daughters got him drunk and had sex with him so they could have children	FF. Joshua 7
___ ___	G. Eutychus	7. A shadow moved *backward* to prove to this person God's promise of fifteen more years to live	GG. Joshua 10:12-14
___ ___	H. Gomer	8. While winning victories for God, he told the sun to stand still until he could wrap up a battle	HH. Judges 4:17-21
___ ___	I. Haman	9. She was a prostitute who married a prophet	II. II Kings 5:8-14
___ ___	J. Herod	10. Became "angry enough to die" when a worm killed his shade plant	JJ. II Kings 9:30-37
___ ___	K. Hezekiah	11. Took credit for being a god, was struck down by the real God, and was eaten by worms	KK. II Kings 13:20, 21
___ ___	L. Isaiah	12. Dogs devoured all of this evil person's body except for skull, feet, and hands	LL. II Kings 20:1-11
___ ___	M. Jael	13. Was cured of leprosy by dipping seven times in the Jordan River	MM. Esther 7
___ ___	N. Jeremiah	14. Saw God on His throne, surrounded by flying, six-winged angels	NN. Isaiah 6:1-8
___ ___	O. Jezebel	15. Said God's people would be taken captive, so he was thrown into a mud pit	OO. Jeremiah 38:1-6
___ ___	P. Jonah	16. Secretly stole spoils of victory and caused his whole army to lose its next battle	PP. Hosea 1:2, 3
___ ___	Q. Joshua	17. Had a staff that budded, blossomed, and produced almonds—overnight!	QQ. Jonah 4:5-9
___ ___	R. Leah	18. Was mistaken for Zeus by people in Lystra	RR. Acts 12:21-23
___ ___	S. Lot	19. Took sister's place in wedding and spent honeymoon night with husband before he noticed	SS. Acts 14:8-18
___ ___	T. Naaman	20. His evil plan backfired, and he was hanged on his own gallows	TT. Acts 20:7-12

NO MR E

Suppose you're going out cruising, driving your BMW (big mule Wilma). You're cruising the Bible expressway, where you almost always see a number of "celebrities." You can't always see their faces because of the bright sun, the veils, and the tinted glass. But the way you can tell who they are is by their personalized license plates. Here a donkey, there a camel, and occasionally a chariot goes by. You've collected the following plate numbers. How many of these Bible characters can you identify? (We also left a few blank to let you create some customized plates for other Bible characters you can think of.)

1. NIK AT NIT
2. STON 2 4HD
3. WMN JDG
4. H20 WLKR
5. ME N BOAZ
6. GR8 FLUD
7. WISEGUY
8. SLNGSHOT
9. FSH 8 ME
10. 2 MCH HAIR
11. UPATREE
12. DED 4 DAYS
13. OLLLLLD
14.
15.

EXTRA ACTION

Step 1
Begin the session with an indoor scavenger hunt. Create a list of items that might be found in the place where you're meeting. If you're in a church, for example, your list might include a bulletin that's over two months old, a piece of lost-and-found clothing, a little kid's drawing, a gum wrapper, a used coffee cup, any item that has been used in a Christmas play, a cassette tape of a sermon or speaker, and so forth. Have group members form teams. Make copies of your list, provide each team with a copy, and begin the hunt. After a designated time, call everyone back together and see which team has collected the most items. Later in the session, compare the fun of searching for hard-to-find items with the potential thrill of discovering portions of the Bible that have been previously "undiscovered."

Step 2
Rather than having group members complete Repro Resource 7 as written, use the list of names as material for charades. Have group members form teams. Instruct each team to designate one person as the clue giver. Advise teams to choose someone who knows the Bible pretty well to give the clues (and make sure each team has one or two such people). The clue giver may have to do some quick matching of people and events to figure out some of the connections. Encourage the clue givers not to linger too long on any name that his or her teammates seem unaware of. After a while, call time and see which team guessed the most names correctly. Then go down the list of names and see which ones, if any, stumped your teams. Continue your discussion with the questions provided in the session.

SMALL GROUP

Step 1
The smaller your group is, the less exciting the opening activity will be. A better option might be a "guess who wrote this" contest. Distribute index cards and pencils. Ask three of the questions from the session, and have kids write down their answers. Then collect what the cards, read them one at a time, and let group members guess who wrote what. Usually this activity reveals some surprises about several group members and helps them get to know one another better.

Step 3
If a sword drill doesn't promise to be very thrilling due to the shortage of competitors, divide the group members into two teams. Assign each team half of the Bible references you would have used for the sword drill. Then have a contest to see which team can find all of its verses first. However, in addition to finding the verses, team members must write a brief explanation as to why each one is meaningful. The explanation must be written out before a team gets credit for finding the verse. When both teams have finished finding their passages, declare a winner. Then go through the list and discuss each passage, letting team members share what they found.

LARGE GROUP

Step 1
An alternative to the opening activity is to play "To Tell the Truth." Choose three volunteers at a time. Meet with your volunteers, and have them discuss unusual events from their past that no one else in the group would know about. Decide which volunteer's story is most unusual. Explain that each volunteer is to try to convince the group that he or she is the one who experienced that particular situation. The real person, of course, can simply tell the truth. The other two will need to do some creative bluffing and acting to try to convince the group. You should announce the situation to the group: **One of these three people, at the age of four, played "Chopsticks" for a Senator of the United States** (or whatever)**.** Other kids will be allowed to ask a few questions. (Who was the Senator? What state were you living in at the time? How does the melody to "Chopsticks" go?) Your two bluffers will need to think quickly to answer the questions. After three or four questions, have kids vote as to which person they think is telling the truth. Try several sets of volunteers and situations to see who is best at bluffing. Then use these "secrets" from people's pasts to lead into the session goal of finding new discoveries in Scripture that may have been "hidden" until now.

Step 4
Writing out and discussing all of the possible solutions to problems may take too long in a large group. Instead, after you come up with a list of reasons why people remain unaware of so much that's in Scripture, deal with each problem in a more immediate manner. One at a time, single out a problem and ask three kids to give you advice on how to deal with it in order to be more aware of the Bible's teachings. Then have other kids evaluate each person's advice by applauding. The person who receives the loudest applause should be the one with the best advice.

HEARD IT ALL BEFORE

Step 2
Prior to the meeting, find an assortment of Bible trivia books that vary in difficulty. Before you hand out copies of Repro Resource 7, have a contest to see who can get the most questions right before missing one. Start with some of the easier questions. (Try to bring out the "heard it all before" attitude of your members.) Then gradually increase the difficulty of the questions. Eventually move into the very difficult questions that no one but Bible scholars would know. Help demonstrate to your group members that there is always more to learn about Scripture. "Trivia" is only one aspect of Bible knowledge, yet the Bible is so complex that it is difficult to maintain a knowledge of even the basic *facts*. Beyond that, a more important goal should be to put into practice the things we know.

Step 5
After group members complete Repro Resource 8, have them form teams for "The License Plate Game." Instruct the teams to create license plates for Bible characters (other than the ones mentioned on Repro Resource 8). The license plates should provide sufficient clues as to the character's identity, yet should be clever enough to stump the other team(s). Set a time limit for guessing for each license plate. If the character's identity isn't guessed within the time limit, the team that came up with the idea gets a point. If the character's identity is guessed, the team that guesses gets a point. A group that knows the Bible fairly well should be able to draw on a number of characters and have a wide variety of creative license plates. If you can channel your group members' "Been there; heard that; what's next?" attitude into challenging games and other creative outlets, they may discover they still have much to learn.

LITTLE BIBLE BACKGROUND

Step 1
It's difficult to conduct a session about obscure Bible stories for kids who may not be aware of many of the major ones. So you might want to start by seeing exactly how much your group members *do* know. Ask the following questions:
• How many of the Ten Commandments can you name?
• How many of the twelve disciples can you name?
• How many of the twenty-seven New Testament books can you name?
• How many of the thirty-nine Old Testament books can you name?
• How many miracles of Jesus can you name?

Your group members may know more than they think. If so, they should be encouraged, and you can move on. If not, you may want to spend more time on some of the "basic" stories of the Bible, rather than trying to cover lesser-known ones.

Step 2
Repro Resource 7 is likely to contain a lot of stories your group members don't know. Rather than creating a lot of confusion by trying to do the sheet as written, have kids focus on the events only. As a group, determine the three events on the sheet that sound most interesting. Then have kids form three groups. Assign each group one of the three events, as well as the Bible reference for that event. Instruct the groups to look up their assigned passages and prepare a brief report on their assigned event. While group members will only get a "sampling" of the tucked-away stories in the Bible, it will be better for them to go home knowing three of them than to still be ignorant about them all.

FELLOWSHIP & WORSHIP

Step 2
After group members have matched all of the columns on Repro Resource 7, explain that you want them to make a few more "matches." Challenge them to match other group members (and themselves) with stories they think best describe each person's personality. For example, can they see any of their peers in Balaam's place, having an "intelligent" conversation with an animal? Could any of the girls pick up a hammer and a stake to defend her nation against an evil enemy? Are any of the guys likely to be mistaken for gods? Have group members focus only on positive stories—not the ones that deal with biblical villains. Try to create a greater sense of fellowship using positive speculation. This activity should encourage group members to recognize unique traits about each other. And once such traits begin to be identified, friendships can begin to develop and grow at deeper levels.

Step 3
As you discuss the importance of ongoing Bible study, perhaps several of your group members would be willing to commit to putting extra effort into seeing what the Bible has to say. If so, form a small study group of those who would like to give it a try. Give them a few minutes to discuss what they would like to study. (This session should provide them with a lot of possibilities.) Then help them get started, giving them suggestions on where to meet, how to conduct the study, and so forth. If a lot of group members are interested, you might want to consider having an additional group meeting every week. The regular group can continue with its emphasis on fun, personal commitment to God, and evangelistic outreach. The new group could then focus almost entirely on Bible knowledge and spiritual growth. Many groups have members who are ready to commit to more than they can get out of "regular" meetings, and this may be the opportunity they're looking for.

MOSTLY GIRLS

Step 2

Distribute index cards and pencils. Have your girls write down several things about themselves that no one else knows. Assure them that these are for their eyes only. Then explain that just as we all have things about us that no one (or very few people) know, there are also "hidden" parts of the Bible that many people aren't aware of. Say: **Though we may not want others to know these hidden parts of ourselves, God wants us to know *all* parts of the Bible. He attempts to hide *nothing* from us. In fact, the more we know of the Bible, the better!**

Step 3

Some of your girls may admit that they're not sure how to examine what they read. (And if there aren't any who'll admit it publicly, you can be sure there are some who are thinking it.) Take a few minutes to talk about what it means to "examine" Scripture. Then brainstorm a list of general questions your group members can ask themselves about a passage. Examples might include the following: "How does this relate to my life?" "Who wrote this?" "To whom was it addressed?" "Why was it written?" "What's the main point the author wants to get across?"

MOSTLY GUYS

Step 2

Rather than discuss all of the random stories on Repro Resource 7, this might be a good time to cover some obscure stories that could be embarrassing to deal with in mixed company. For example, the stories of Dinah and the Shechemites (Genesis 34) and Lot's daughters (Genesis 19:30-38) are both on the sheet. But there are also interesting (and sensitive) stories about Judah and Tamar (Genesis 38); Abraham, Sarah, and Abimelech (Genesis 20); Jephthah's foolish vow (Judges 11); a Levite and his concubine (Judges 19–21); Absalom and Tamar (II Samuel 13); and many more. Pay particular attention to biblical accounts of loutish male behavior. Challenge your group members to take note of such actions (and their consequences) and avoid making the same mistakes.

Step 4

The average teenage guy may not like to admit to the need for Bible study. Yet few can argue that it's not important. Perhaps some guys simply need to begin with something that interests *them*. To help find appropriate portions of Scripture where they might begin to do daily devotions, have each person describe someone he would consider a personal hero. The "hero" might be a sports figure, musician, family member, or anyone. In each case, have group members decide what specific qualities of the person are most admirable. Then, as a group, try to identify Bible stories of people with those same characteristics. Give each group member some ideas of people to look up and read about who come closest to fitting the descriptions of their personal heroes. Bible study might take on a whole new fascination if your guys can find the right starting point.

EXTRA FUN

Step 1

Play "The Obscurity Game." Let group members take turns naming categories. For each category, kids should try to think of the most obscure thing that fits the category. Categories might include things like countries, state capitols, dog breeds, insects, languages, Beatles songs, musical instruments, and so forth. Award small prizes to the people who come up with the most obscure answers for the different categories. For your final category, have each group member name what he or she thinks is the most obscure Bible story. List group members answers on the board. Later, compare their answers with the stories listed on Repro Resource 7.

Step 5

Find the game Bible Outburst™ (© 1989 Hersch & Company) or create your own version. The object of the game is to guess as many items as possible on a category card. For example, one category from the game is "People in the Old Testament Who Saw Angels." The ten names given on the card are (1) Hagar, (2) Abraham, (3) Lot, (4) Balaam, (5) Gideon, (6) Elijah, (7) Daniel, (8) Zechariah, (9) David, and (10) Samson's parents. These aren't the only people in the Old Testament who saw angels, but they're the only ones players can get credit for. One point is awarded for each of the listed people that players can name. A few other categories from the game are "Famous Pairs of People in the New Testament," "Names in the Bible Beginning with O," "People Associated with John the Baptist," and "Plagues Sent on the Egyptians." Most of the cards have ten possible answers. If you can't obtain a copy of the game, you can create enough of your own cards to play. This is a good way to get into some additional "minutia" of the Bible and conclude the session with some fun and excitement.

OPTIONS

S E S S I O N   F O U R

MEDIA

Step 4

An alternative to the tabloid assignment at the end of Step 4 is the video equivalent. If you have a video camera, and if your kids are more inclined to enjoy visual and verbal presentations of material rather than printed ones, let them create TV newsmagazines and send teams out to "cover" some of the biblical miracles. Some of the team members will play the roles of the newscaster and reporters. Others will play the roles of participants and eyewitnesses to the miracles. Give the teams a few minutes to prepare their material. Then, as each team gives its report, videotape the presentation. After all of the teams have reported, play back the tape, and let group members watch themselves.

Step 5

The license plate activity on Repro Resource 8 might be just a starting point for media-minded group members. Another fun exercise would be to come up with titles of biographies (or autobiographies) for Bible characters. Have a list of recent best-selling biographies to give kids some ideas (*Me* by Katherine Hepburn, *Rare Air* about Michael Jordan, *I Had a Hammer* by Hank Aaron, and so forth). Then have group members think of Bible characters and what their life stories might be titled.

SHORT MEETING TIME

Step 2

One way to condense the meeting time of this session is to use the two Repro Resources as the main portion of the lesson. Repro Resource 7 provides a number of potential Bible stories to follow up on after group members do the initial match-ups. Repro Resource 8 provides a creative exercise with which to wrap up the session. If time permits, end your meeting time with the problem-solving exercise in Step 4 to give group members the opportunity to share problems they face in regard to Bible study, and to receive some good suggestions to try.

Step 5

Replace Step 5 with a shorter activity. After your group members have been inundated with story after story and character after character, it might be a good idea to let them try to put some of the pieces together. Challenge each person in your group to write the names of four characters in the Bible who are all somehow related or who all have something in common—except for one. In other words, three of the characters should have some "tie that binds"; the fourth shouldn't. The task of the rest of the group is to guess which character doesn't belong and explain why. Give group members a few minutes to come up with their four characters. Then, one at a time, have kids read their list of names to the group. If no one can correctly guess within fifteen seconds which character doesn't belong, award a prize to the person who came up with the list. A sample list might include Ahab, Boaz, Solomon, and Saul. The one who doesn't belong is Boaz, who wasn't a king like the others. (You might find that kids come up with different answers that also work. That's OK.)

URBAN

Step 2

After you go through Repro Resource 7, have your group members consider who are some of the less-familiar "heroes" in your church. Of course, everyone sees the pastor, the choir director, the organist, and the ushers. But what about the behind-the-scenes people like the custodian, the church bus (or van) driver, or the pastor's secretary? How much recognition do they get? Take a few moments at this point in the session to write brief thank-you cards to the "unsung heroes" in your church.

Step 3

Instead of using the sword-drill activity, have your group members focus on one or more specific themes or topics in the Bible. Here are a few ideas to get you started:

- *Women in the Bible*—Sarah (Genesis 11–23); Lot's wife (Genesis 19:26); Rebekah (Genesis 24–27); Rachel and Leah (Genesis 29–35); Miriam (Exodus 2:1-10); Rahab (Joshua 2–6); Ruth and Naomi (Ruth 1–4); Esther (Esther 1–9); etc.
- *Laughter in the Bible*—Genesis 17:17; 18:12-14; 21:6; Job 8:21; Psalm 2:4; 37:13; 126:2; Proverbs 14:13; Ecclesiastes 2:2; 3:4; Luke 6:21
- *African presence in the Bible*—Ethiopians and Cushites (Genesis 10:6-9; Numbers 12:1; II Chronicles 14:9-13; 16:8; Jeremiah 13:23; Amos 9:7; Acts 8:27); Egypt/Egyptians (Genesis 15:18; 21:9; 45:19; Exodus 1–14; Psalm 78:12; Acts 21:38); Simon of Cyrene (Mark 15:21; Luke 23:26)

JR. HIGH / HIGH SCHOOL COMBINED

Step 1
It may be difficult to know how much Bible knowledge your younger group members have accumulated. So rather than doing the opening activity in Step 1, try an exercise that will give you some clues. Distribute paper and pencils. Then say: **I'm going to name an object. You should then write down all of the Bible stories you know that deal with that object. For example, if I were to say, "Stone," you might write down David and Goliath, Jesus' resurrection—when the stone was rolled away from the tomb, Abraham's altar on which he offered Isaac, the stoning of Stephen, and so forth. For every story you think of, you get a point. For every story you think of that no one else thinks of, you get five points.** Start with some basic objects to see how well group members do. If they seem to be doing well, you can try some less common ones. For example, you might start out with *boat, fish, sword, bird, river,* etc. Later you might try *arrow, chariot, robe,* etc. Use a concordance if you need some additional ideas. As group members share their lists (and you add your own input), you should be able to tell how well most of your kids know the Bible, and you'll be able to lead the session more effectively.

Step 2
Some of the stories included on Repro Resource 7 may be too intense or "mature" for younger group members. If you feel this could be a problem for your group, you need not hand out copies of the sheet. Instead, you can read selected events from the sheet and let group members try to identify the person involved with the event. You can also add other stories your group members should know to replace the ones you eliminate. The verbal presentation of Repro Resource should go quickly, so you might want to add quite a few names and events.

EXTRA CHALLENGE

Step 3
Perhaps your group members are already devoted to regular Bible reading. If so, give them the additional challenge of Bible memorization. But instead of the "big" verses of Scripture, encourage group members to memorize passages that are special to *them* in some way. Sometimes in reading a lesser-known passage, a verse or group of verses may seem to jump out as being very important. These may be verses your group members will never hear quoted or preached on. But if they seem important to the individuals doing the reading, they are certainly worth memorizing and remembering. Encourage your group members not to be so intent on quantity of reading. Make sure they are learning at a pace that allows the truths of the Bible to soak in and be recalled when needed.

Step 5
If your group (or certain individuals) are exceptionally motivated, you might want to challenge them to begin a read-through-the-Bible program. It takes quite a commitment to read though the Bible in a single year, so you might want to consider some two-year (or longer) programs. Your local Christian bookstore will probably have some resources that will help you. If your kids don't think they have the time or energy to read through the Bible, you might want to provide them with less intensive projects (such as a verse-a-day calendar, good devotional books, etc.).

PLANNING CHECKLIST

Date Used:

Approx. Time

Step 1: The Match Game ______
o Extra Action
o Small Group
o Large Group
o Little Bible Background
o Extra Fun
o Combined Jr. High/High School

Step 2: The Second String ______
o Extra Action
o Heard It All Before
o Little Bible Background
o Fellowship & Worship
o Mostly Girls
o Mostly Guys
o Short Meeting Time
o Urban
o Combined Jr. High/High School

Step 3: Books and Crannies ______
o Small Group
o Fellowship & Worship
o Mostly Girls
o Urban
o Extra Challenge

Step 4: Too Much of a Good Thing? ______
o Large Group
o Mostly Guys
o Media

Step 5: Taking the Study Out of Bible Study ______
o Heard It All Before
o Extra Fun
o Media
o Short Meeting Time
o Extra Challenge

SESSION

5 Behold! A Mystery!

YOUR GOALS FOR THIS SESSION:

Choose one or more

- [ ] To help kids see that all parts of the Bible are important—even those that deal with "mundane" issues such as census figures, genealogies, and strange prophecies.
- [ ] To help kids understand that like any other mystery, we need to search for clues to help us discover certain biblical truths that may not be as obvious as others.
- [ ] To help kids experience the satisfaction of solving a biblical mystery while in the group, and to challenge them to continue to try to do so on their own.
- [ ] Other ______________________

Your Bible Base:

Daniel 2
Various passages that deal with the "mysteries" of Scripture

STEP 1

It's a Mystery to Me

(Needed: Trivia book, slips of paper prepared according to instructions)

OPTIONS

Before the session, try to find a book that gives explanations for a number of odd occurrences. Select several good questions to pose to group members—questions for which the answers aren't too long or complicated. Photocopy the correct answer for each question.

To begin the session, call for several volunteers. Each volunteer will draw a slip of paper. One slip should have the answer to your question. The others should be blank. Ask the question aloud and give your volunteers time to think of an answer. (You might want to have them turn their backs so the person with the actual answer can read it without being obvious.) Those who have blank slips of paper should make up answers and try to bluff. The person with the actual answer should paraphrase his or her response so it sounds like he or she is making it up.

If you don't have a good book available, here are a few sample questions. (These are taken from the popular Imponderables™ series by David Feldman, published by HarperCollins. A couple of titles in the series are *Why Do Dogs Have Wet Noses?* and *When Did Wild Poodles Roam the Earth?*)

- **What does the "Q" in "Q-Tips" stand for?** (Quality.)
- **Why do you so often see tires on top of mobile homes in trailer parks?** (They prevent wind from causing the roof to pop in and out, and they reduce the noise of rain and hail.)
- **Why are paper and plastic drinking cups wider at the top than the bottom, when that makes them easier to tip over? Why not make them more like bottles?** (They need to be nested inside each other to be marketed effectively.)
- **Why do pretzels have such a strange shape?** (They were invented by a monk to reward good students. The shape was meant to resemble the arms of a child in prayer.)
- **Why do ironworkers wear their hard hats backward?** (They wear goggles much of the time and don't have to remove their hats to pull up the goggles onto their foreheads.)
- **What are male gnats doing when they swarm?** (They are males looking for female companionship.)
- **How did the grandfather clock get its name?** (From a song: "My grandfather's clock was too long for the shelf, so it stood ninety

years on the floor.")

After each question, have your volunteers give their answers. Then let the rest of the group members vote for which person they think is telling the truth. Do this several times with new volunteers. See who can get the most votes for a made-up answer.

After playing for a while, point out that it is possible to have some fun, even when dealing with difficult questions. Then ask: **On a scale of one to ten—with ten being the most—how curious would you say you are about finding out why things work the way they do? In other words, do you tend to accept things as they are without questioning, or do you use the phrase, "I wonder why . . ." a lot?** The responses of your group members are likely to provide clues to their approach to Bible study. Group members who aren't naturally curious may not attempt to deal with prophetic passages or hard-to-understand portions of Scripture. They may simply move on to material that is easier to understand. The curious people, however, will take a different approach. They are likely to try to dig deeper. This can result in enthusiasm when they figure out a difficult passage, but potential frustration when they can't.

STEP 2

Clanging Symbols

(Needed: Bibles, copies of Repro Resource 9, pencils)

Before you deal with the issue of biblical symbolism, introduce the topic from a secular perspective. Explain: **Everyone needs to learn to struggle with symbolism. Classic literature is filled with symbols, similes, metaphors, and other words and phrases that aren't literal. We cannot read *Aesop's Fables,* Shakespeare's plays, or most poems and novels without having to put some thought into what the author is really trying to say. At first reading, *Moby Dick* may seem like the story of a man and a whale. But few college book reports will allow such a limited perspective of what Melville was trying to express. When Shakespeare wrote that "All the world's a stage," he didn't mean that *literally*. We have to put some brain cells to work to make the connection he intended us to make. So a personal dislike for symbolism is no reason to stop trying to figure out the portions of the Bible that aren't**

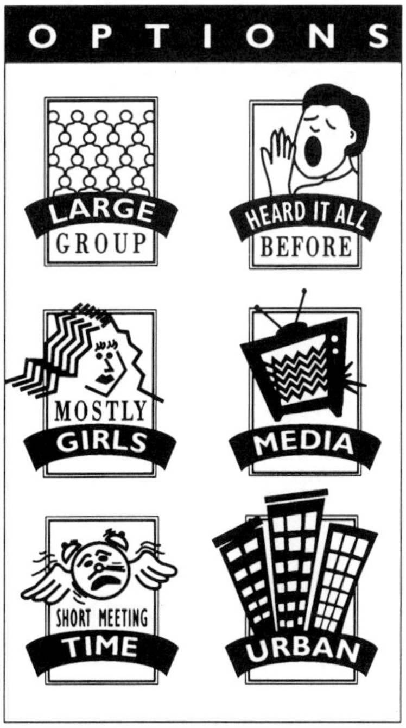

as clear as others.

How many symbolic passages can you think of in the Bible? (Jesus' parables, much of the Book of Revelation, a lot of Old Testament imagery, etc.)

Do you ever have trouble figuring out the symbolism of these passages? Sometimes the symbolism is explained in the text itself. Sometimes we can figure out for ourselves. Other times we may guess, but be unsure about what the symbols mean.

Besides symbolic passages, what other portions of Scripture do you find difficult or perhaps irrelevant? (Genealogies, census figures, precise weights and measurements, etc.)

Why do you think all of these things are contained in the Bible? Point out that they are all there for a good reason. Sometimes we can figure out the reasons. Other times we may need to wait to discover the purpose of such passages.

If you don't understand such things, why not simply skip over them and move on to a different part of the Bible? (While these things are certainly not the most interesting or dynamic portions of Scripture and may not demand a high percentage of our Bible study time, we will never make sense of them unless we *occasionally* try to figure out why they are there.)

Explain: **God sometimes uses mysteries on purpose. If we refuse to struggle mentally with those things, we will never understand them. But if we "play detective" and look for clues, we will eventually begin to make sense of them.** If you've already done Session 3 in this book, remind kids of Matthew 13:12: "Whoever has will be given more, and he will have an abundance. Whoever does not have, even what he has will be taken from him."

Hand out copies of "One Good Mystery Deserves Another" (Repro Resource 9) and pencils. Group members are asked to figure out a number of mysteries, each of which should reveal a reference to a *biblical* "mystery." (You may want to have kids work in teams to complete the sheet.) When they finish, they should have "deciphered" and read the following passages and the mysteries that are described.

- Matthew 13:11—We can know the "secrets" of the kingdom of heaven.
- Romans 11:25—The way that God provided salvation for the Gentiles as well as the Jewish people was a mystery to the Jewish people for a while.
- I Corinthians 2:7-10—The work of God and His love for His people is a mystery to those who don't know Him.
- I Corinthians 15:51, 52—The transformation that living Christians will undergo at Jesus' return is a mystery.
- Ephesians 1:9, 10—God's will and purpose are a mystery to many, but have been revealed to His people.

• Ephesians 5:31, 32—The "husband-wife" connection between Christ and the church is a mysterious relationship.

• Colossians 1:27—One mystery God's people learn to understand is "Christ in you, the hope of glory."

• I Timothy 3:16—The "mystery of godliness" is that sinful people can be made righteous through the incarnation and work of Jesus.

• Revelation 10:7—God's eventual and ultimate triumph over evil is a mystery yet to be realized.

Explain that these are by no means all of the verses that refer to the "mysteries" of God. As you can see, like any good mystery, most of these things *can* be understood. We start out confused and in the dark. But in most cases, we have been provided enough clues to follow so that if we *try*, we can solve the "mystery." In a few instances, we may not find the answer. Yet that shouldn't prevent us from waiting and searching.

STEP 3

In Your Dreams

(Needed: Bibles)

Ask: **What is the number one thing that needs to happen before we can understand the mysteries of God?** Although you've been discussing the need for effort on *our* part, even more important is God's willingness to reveal such things to us. If He didn't want us to know something, we could never figure it out on our own. (See James 1:5-8.)

Perhaps nowhere is this made clearer than in Daniel 2. It's a lengthy chapter, but not difficult to understand. And it will go quickly if you assign "parts" and read it as a play. One person should be a narrator who reads all portions that are not quotations. Other parts are King Nebuchadnezzar, astrologers (several), Daniel, and Arioch (who speaks only in verse 25).

Stop the action after verses 1-13 have been read and make sure everyone is clear on the facts. King Nebuchadnezzar has had a dream, and he wants his wise men to interpret it—*before* he tells them what the dream was. If they can tell the king his dream and its interpretation, they get "gifts and rewards and great honor." If they can't, they will be cut into pieces and their houses turned into piles of rubble. The astrologers argued that no man on earth could do such a thing—only "the

gods." But that's not what Nebuchadnezzar wanted to hear, so he passed a death sentence on his staff of wise men. At this time, Daniel—along with Shadrach, Meshach, and Abednego—was on staff as well, but this passage suggests that he and his friends didn't hang out with the other wise men.

Stop the action again after verses 14-23 have been read and review the facts. When Daniel heard what was going on, he didn't panic. Instead, he gathered all of the facts he could and asked the king for a little time. He and his three godly friends then prayed for wisdom. (Hananiah, Mishael, and Azariah are the Hebrew names for Shadrach, Meshach, and Abednego.) That night "the mystery was revealed" to Daniel. And, by the way, the first thing he did was not to go running to the king. First, he stopped and praised God for providing the wisdom he had asked for. (As you read through this portion, you might want to keep a count of how many times God is referred to in connection with revealing mysteries or secret things.)

Stop the action again after verses 24-30 have been read and review the facts. Note that Daniel didn't take a bit of credit for knowing the king's dream and its interpretation. He made it very clear that the revelation came from the one God in heaven. He refers to God as "the revealer of mysteries."

You can skip the content of the dream (vss. 31-45) if you wish. While this story is a key prophetic passage and is usually the portion of Daniel 2 that people pay attention to, it's more important here to show that God is a "revealer of mysteries" in general—not specifically for Nebuchadnezzar. But be sure to focus on the king's reaction in verses 46-49. Nebuchadnezzar became convinced that Daniel served "the God of gods and the Lord of kings and a revealer of mysteries." In addition, Daniel and his friends were given positions of power in Nebuchadnezzar's kingdom.

Summarize: **Daniel truly believed that God was a revealer of mysteries, and his belief literally saved his life. While we seldom face immediate life-or-death situations to test our faith, we would certainly do better to have faith that God will help us understand "mysterious" portions of Scripture that initially confuse us.**

STEP 4

Why Bother?

(Needed: Bibles, copies of Repro Resource 10)

As you were reading Daniel 2, did anyone question who "Hananiah, Mishael, and Azariah" were (vs. 17)? Or why they had two names? (See Daniel 1:6, 7.) These are the kinds of questions group members need to begin to ask if the Bible is ever going to make more sense to them.

Hand out copies of "Elementary, My Dear Methuselah" (Repro Resource 10). Have kids work on the biblical mystery: Did Methuselah die in the flood? (Answer: Methuselah had Lamech at age 187. Lamech had Noah at age 182. The flood came when Noah was 600. So 187 + 182 + 600 = 969, the age of Methuselah when he died.) This exercise should help group members see that there is some significance to the "begats" of the Bible. While we may tend to pass them over, sometimes we miss important clues by doing so.

Spend a few minutes letting kids express what they think are the least meaningful portions of the Bible. Then ask for reasons why such parts of Scripture might actually be important. Here are three common answers, with a few suggestions to explain the value of each one.

Genealogies

You might want to use Jesus' genealogies (Matthew 1:1-17; Luke 3:23-38) as examples. Group members should be able to see names they recognize: Abraham, Isaac, Jacob, Ruth and Boaz, David, Solomon, etc. While their stories are good ones, their history should mean even more when we realize they were leading up to the birth of the Savior of the world. You'll also find Rahab (see Joshua 2), a pagan prostitute who, along with her family, was spared death because she placed her faith in God. The significance of her presence in the line of Jesus should not go unnoticed.

Prophecy

Have group members thumb through the hundreds of pages from Isaiah to Malachi. Explain that the prophets were warning about (or living through) the captivity of God's people. They had much to say about the sins of His people as well as those of surrounding nations—and the whole bit may seem confusing and boring. Yet tucked away in those hundreds of pages are hundreds of wonderful promises (Jeremiah 33:3), hopes (Habakkuk 3:17, 18), prophecies of Jesus (Isaiah 9; 11), and stories of God's awesome love and provision for His people (Daniel and Jonah, to name just a couple).

OPTIONS

LITTLE BIBLE BACKGROUND

MOSTLY GUYS

JR. HIGH HIGH SCHOOL COMBINED

EXTRA CHALLENGE

Old Testament Laws .

Sometimes people determine to read through the Bible, and they do reasonably well with Genesis and Exodus. But the Leviticus-Numbers-Deuteronomy trio of Old Testament law is enough to stop many of them in their tracks. Yet until we get a good sense of the burden it would be to live "under the law," we cannot truly appreciate what it means to live in God's grace. We also get a better understanding of the importance of *love* because Jesus sums up the entire Old Testament law in two commands: (1) Love God completely, and (2) Love our neighbors as ourselves (Mark 12:28-31). If our level of love ever got to where it *should* be, we wouldn't need all of those laws. Also, the books of law are filled with images that point to the coming of Jesus (blood sacrifices, priestly intercession, the bronze snake in the wilderness, etc.).

Your group members may come up with other portions of Scripture that don't exactly thrill them. But in each case, try to show how those portions are necessary to give us a more complete picture of God's active work among mankind. Such passages may be very mysterious now. But none of them are too hard to understand if we are willing to do a little "digging." The Gospels and other New Testament sections may seem much more relevant. Yet they are even more so when we have a good understanding of the "mysterious" portions of Scripture that are related to them.

STEP 5

Hope in the Dark

Ask: **Do you think God wants us to know *everything* He knows?** Obviously, we aren't capable of knowing all that God knows. Yet group members may come to the realization that God is always willing to teach us something new—much more than we usually attempt to know.

Continue: **When you are trying to figure something out, and you just can't seem to do it no matter how hard you try, how is your faith affected? Do you ever assume God just doesn't care? Or that you must not be "spiritual enough"?** Let group members respond.

Then explain: **God is the one and only source for true wisdom, so we need to seek His help when we come across portions of the Bible we don't understand. However, our**

faith should not depend on getting answers to every question we might have. For example, one of the biggest mysteries of the Bible is when Jesus will return. People create all sorts of theories and wild guesses, and sometimes convince a lot of others to believe them. Yet Jesus Himself told His disciples, "No one knows about that day or hour, not even the angels in heaven, nor the Son, but only the Father" (Matthew 24:36).

As you can see, some things are mysteries simply because God is not yet ready to reveal them. No matter how hard we study or how much we try, we just won't figure them out—because we can't. But that shouldn't prevent us from searching the Scriptures and learning everything we can.

Close by having someone read aloud Romans 5:3-5: "We also rejoice in our sufferings, because we know that suffering produces perseverance; perseverance, character; and character, hope. And hope does not disappoint us, because God has poured out his love into our hearts by the Holy Spirit, whom he has given us."

Explain that while this promise holds true for any kind of suffering, in this case we can apply it to our struggles to understand the unclear portions of the Bible. If we struggle a bit, we learn to persevere. As we refuse to quit, we develop stronger character. And the end result of this process is that we develop a sure and certain hope that God will see us through any situation—whether we understand it or not.

OPTIONS

ONE GOOD MYSTERY DESERVES ANOTHER

Sometimes during Bible study you may discover that if you figure out one thing, a lot of other mysteries fall into place as well. But other times, you may solve one mystery only to discover that it leads to new ones. The puzzles that follow are from the latter category. If you can figure them out, each reference you discover should lead you to a biblical mystery. First, solve the puzzles to discover the appropriate Bible references. Then look up the references and make a list of the biblical mysteries you find.

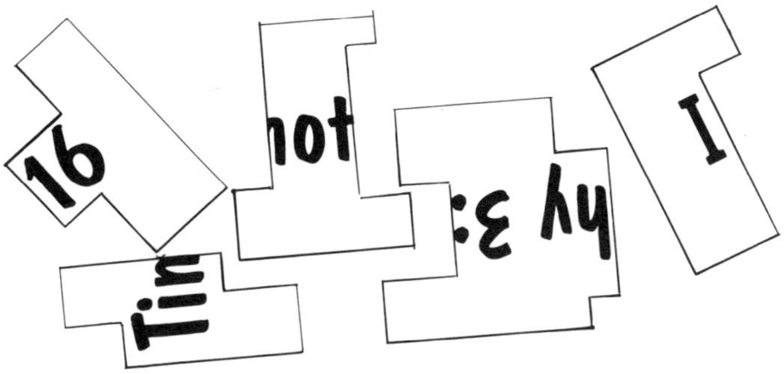

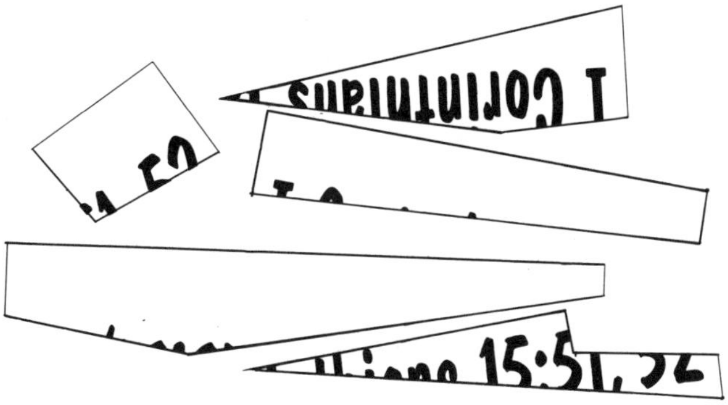

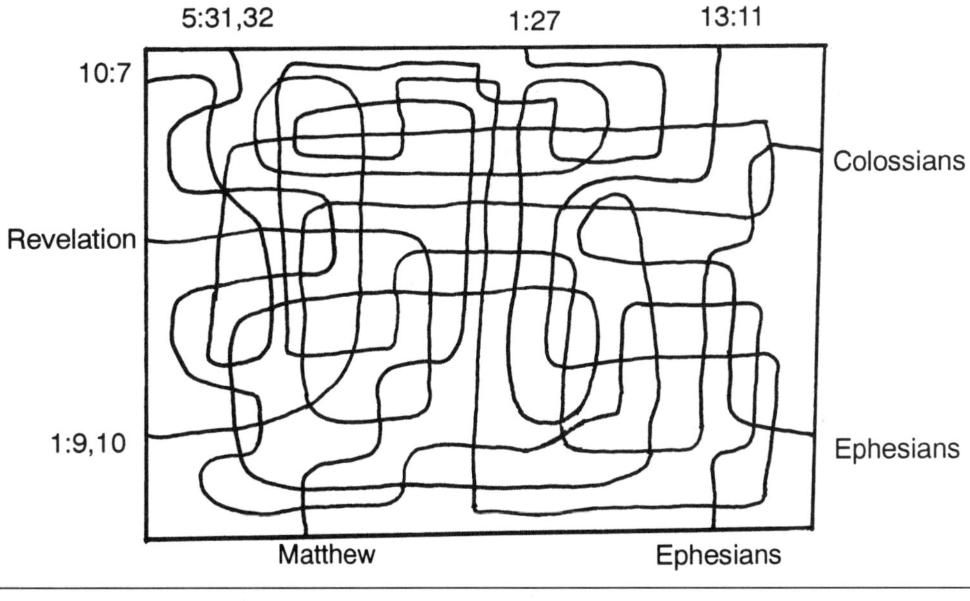

Elementary. My Dear Methuselah

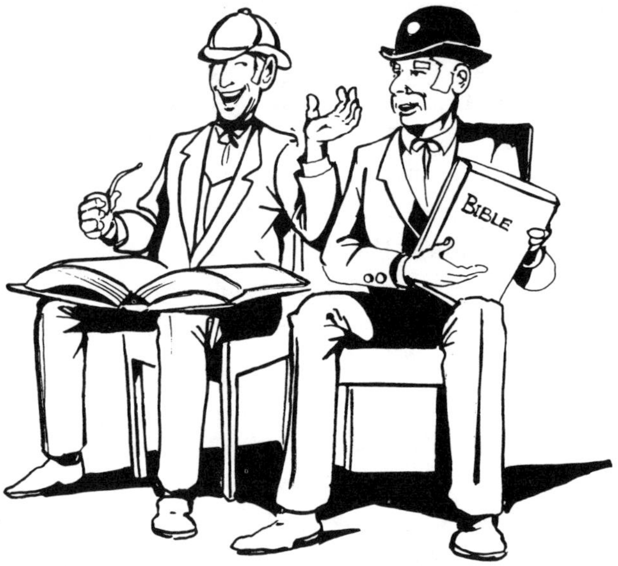

Holmes and Watson were having their daily devotional time (studying Genesis 5–7) when Holmes suddenly spoke: "Watson, do you suppose Methuselah was an evil person?"

Watson replied, "I say, Holmes, you come up with the strangest ideas. Whatever gave you that notion?"

"Because he died during the year of Noah's flood," said Holmes. "So it causes one to wonder."

Watson stared incredulously. "Holmes," he sputtered, "I've read that passage hundreds of times and I can assure you it says nothing about Methuselah dying in the big flood. All anyone knows about Methuselah is that he is the oldest person who ever lived."

"The oldest *recorded* person," corrected Holmes.

"Whatever," said Watson. "But the Bible says nothing about his dying in the great flood. I'm quite sure."

"I must admit," conceded Holmes, "that I cannot prove he died *because of* the flood. But he died that year, so we cannot rule out the possibility. And *if* he died in the flood, he must not have been a righteous person."

"Holmes, you always astound me," said an astounded Watson. "But you must show me how you reached your conclusion."

"It's elementary—if you read the 'begats' portion of the passage and do a little simple math," said Holmes. [NOTE: Holmes and Watson had only the *King James Version* of the Bible to work by, so they read that Methuselah *begat* Lamech and Lamech *begat* Noah.]

Watson confessed, "Ah, so that's it. I always skip those parts."

"You shouldn't," chided Holmes. "If you read Genesis 5:25-30; 7:11, 12, you should come to the same conclusion I reached."

Watson got out a pencil and paper, scratched his head a time or two, and finally said, "I say, Holmes. You've done it again!"

"Elementary, my dear Watson," Holmes replied.

How about you? Can you figure out how Holmes was able to determine that Methuselah died during the year of the great flood?

EXTRA ACTION

Step 1
Have kids form two groups. Each group will create and stage a mystery for the other group to figure out. In brainstorming their mysteries, groups should think of other mysteries they've read or seen on TV. The setting may be strange and exotic. The suspects may be eccentric or normal. The victim might be one of the group members, a teacher at school, or anyone else kids choose. Several people should have motives, and the actual murderer should have an alibi (but one that can be discovered as false if the right suspects are interrogated). Each group should be able to set the scene for its mystery quickly. ("A man is found dead in bed. His butler was the last person to see him alive. The man had two children, both of whom were after his vast fortune, and a business partner whom he suspected of embezzling from the company.") Perhaps one or both of your groups will stage a thrilling experience for the other. But more likely, the result of this exercise will be to see how difficult it is to create a good mystery. Keep this point in mind as you work through the session and affirm that God's mysteries will make sense when we eventually figure them out.

Step 5
Have kids build a human pyramid as you discuss the Romans 5:3-5 passage. When you first mention *suffering* (struggling), ask some of your larger kids to form the bottom level of the pyramid. When you get to *perseverance*, have kids form the next level up. When you mention *character*, add a third level. When you explain that all of these things are necessary to have *hope*, have a person form the top level. Point out that if our "foundational" characteristics aren't solid, neither will be the hope we have. Challenge kids to endure their sufferings, persevere through things they don't enjoy, and develop a stronger character. When those elements of their inner, spiritual "pyramid" are strengthened, their hope will be much more sure and steady.

SMALL GROUP

Step 1
If you really want to make a memorable experience out of your discussion of mysteries, you might want to take some extra time prior to the session and plan a "murder party." Bookstores and toy/game stores usually have a broad assortment of options (including "How to Host a Murder" and other series). The boxed package even contains invitations to send out. (Most murder parties require eight people.) Some have options for dinners you can plan in addition to the mystery itself. Costumes aren't necessary, but they add to the mystique of the problem-solving exercise. After all of the participants have arrived, each is given a booklet to provide clues to reveal to the others (and to alert one of the people that he or she is the real murderer). It usually takes an hour or so to do one of these roleplays, so you might need to make special arrangements in advance to ensure that everyone can be there. It won't work if one of the suspects is missing.

Step 3
Before you read the story of Daniel, Shadrach, Meshach, and Abednego, ask your group members to think of these four guys as a small group of faithful people surrounded by a much larger group of people with no respect for God. (They were also young, so they could be classified as a youth group.) Does the situation sound familiar to them? At each pause you make in the story, discuss these questions: **How did Daniel and his friends handle being outnumbered by other people? Do you think they ever wanted to join the majority? What can we learn from them to have a more successful youth group?** Try to help your group members see that sometimes there are even advantages to being small. (They can know each other better; it's easy to get everyone together and working toward the same goals; during times of crisis, they can easily pull together for support; etc.)

LARGE GROUP

Step 2
Play "Kumquat," in which you think of a word with several definitions, replace the word with "kumquat," and then see how many clues it takes for others to guess what the word is. Start with hard clues and then move to easier ones. For example:

- Everyone has a kumquat.
- You never want to be accused of having two kumquats.
- One of our national monuments consists of four very large stone kumquats.
- A clock has a kumquat.
- You can kumquat the music or do an about-kumquat. (Face)

Here's another:

- To "kumquat" can mean "to put up with."
- You can under-kumquat something, but you can't over-kumquat anything.
- If you want to be noticed, you might kumquat.
- "If you don't kumquat for something, you'll fall for anything."
- A song and a movie are titled "Kumquat by Me." (Stand)

After you play a couple rounds with your kids, have them form teams and come up with some words and clues of their own to try out on the other teams.

Step 5
After you discuss Romans 5:3-5, talk about the *importance* of hope in the lives of your young people. Then designate a "Hope Brigade." Not everyone in your group is likely to have worked through the process enough to be hopeful during trying times. So, as a group, determine some of the people who have. The more spiritually mature and optimistic people in your group should be singled out as possible contacts for other kids who are overwhelmed by stress, temptation, depression, or some other situation in which hope is needed. (The people chosen should be willing volunteers, of course.) If you can't find enough people in your group, provide a list of names and phone numbers of adults for your kids to contact if needed.

Heard It All Before

Step 2

A "heard it all before" attitude can be a detriment to enjoying and understanding mysteries. If someone thinks he or she already knows it all, that person will place very little effort into exploring new possibilities. To demonstrate this, have group members read John 3:1-21 (the story of Nicodemus coming to Jesus). Say: **Nicodemus was an extremely educated person, yet he was confused by what Jesus was saying about being "born again." It was a mystery to him. How did Nicodemus handle his confusion?** Help group members see that Nicodemus kept challenging Jesus and asking very simple questions. He didn't mind sounding stupid. And as a result of his efforts, he was the first person to hear what is certainly the most quoted Bible verse ever (John 3:16). Today we don't think twice about being "born again," but that's only because Nicodemus persisted until he could understand that mystery. We should be less willing to assume we know it all and more eager to question and learn.

Step 5

More than likely, your group members have some questions and doubts, whether or not they're eager to let on. As you conclude, ask: **What do you, as an intelligent person, find hardest to believe about the Bible or Christianity?** You might begin by sharing some of the questions you've struggled with. For example, the emphasis on blood sacrifice might seem strange to many people in this day and age. And certainly we should maintain a sense of wonder as to how God made it possible for people to be swallowed by large fish and vomited up three days later, or to walk on water, or to rise from the dead. If we never question such things, we never appreciate them. Perhaps you can help your group members see that some of the greatest mysteries of the Bible grow out of the simplicity of faith rather than intellectual complexity.

Little Bible Background

Step 3

The concept of God as a "revealer of mysteries" should be an appealing one to young people who know very little about Him or His written Word. So after your discussion of Daniel, ask: **If you truly believe that no question or problem is too difficult for God, what would you like to ask Him?** Some group members may be reluctant to share their questions verbally. If so, have them write down what they would like to know. Collect the questions and discuss each one briefly. You may be able to shed some light on some of their concerns at this point. Others are likely to require longer discussions. But if you can provide *some* help now, you can continue to explore their mysteries together at future sessions.

Step 4

You might want to skip this step altogether with a group that doesn't have much Bible background. But if you use it, you might want to have on hand one or more copies of *Games* magazine. Each issue usually has a feature called "Eyeball Benders," in which common objects are photographed from such unusual perspectives that they become difficult to recognize. Let your group members identify as many of the objects as they can. Then summarize: **It's important to get around to everything the Bible has to teach us—eventually. But we need to start with the basics. We need to know the major stories and learn what we can about the life of Jesus, who reveals to us exactly what God is like** (John 14:9)**. To place too much emphasis on genealogies, prophecy, laws, and such before we learn the basics can cause the Bible to look distorted—like the pictures we just saw. But the whole Bible makes sense when we start with the big "clues" and advance to the other ones later on.**

Fellowship & Worship

Step 3

Biblical mysteries may mean nothing compared to a young person's personal mysteries. Adolescence is a period of change and confusion. So if you want to focus more on fellowship, provide a time for group members to discuss the things they don't understand about themselves or each other. Perhaps relationships are becoming more difficult to figure out. Love and hormonal changes are certainly a mystery to most of us. But since God is a "revealer of mysteries," He should certainly be able to help us figure such things out. Challenge group members to memorize Psalm 139:23, 24. Encourage them to become willing to allow God to "search," "test," "see," and "lead" them. As a result, they should begin to find some answers to their personal mysteries.

Step 5

As wrap up the session, emphasize that it takes a great deal of faith to believe in things we don't understand. Distribute paper and pencils. Instruct group members to write an affirmation of their belief. They should title the affirmation "Faith No Matter What." Some kids may choose to write simply stated personal creeds. Others may create poetic expressions or short musical choruses. The form should be up to the person. The more important factor is the thought group members put into what they write and the content of what is expressed. Explain that since we will never understand *everything* God chooses to do in our lives, we need to learn to increase our levels of faith during confusing times. The sooner we get started, the better off our lives will be.

MOSTLY GIRLS

Step 2

If your girls enjoy parties, you may want to take a few minutes to plan a "mystery party." (How-to kits for such parties are available wherever games are sold.) Throwing such a party, in which guests are assigned characters and clues (from which a mystery is solved throughout the course of the party), may help your girls discover how much fun solving a mystery can be. After a few minutes of planning, say: **Speaking of mysteries, let's take a look at some Bible puzzlers.** Lead in to a discussion on the "mysteries" of the Bible.

Step 3

Ask: **Have you ever faced a situation that seemed as impossible as the one Daniel faced? If so, what was it?** Your girls may mention anything from a seemingly impossible school assignment to struggles they've faced at home. Ask them to describe how they got through the situation. Did God intervene as dramatically as He did for Daniel? This topic could lead to an insightful discussion on the many ways God works in our lives (bringing help through other people, giving us a peaceful spirit in trying times, etc.).

MOSTLY GUYS

Step 3

After you go through the story of Daniel's interpretation of King Nebuchadnezzar's dream, ask some tongue-in-cheek questions to your guys: **Where are the women in this story? Where was Daniel's mom, reminding him to say his prayers? Where was Abednego's wife, waking him up to make sure he went to church and became a better person? Is it really possible that a bunch of young guys could move away from home and continue to mature spiritually without begging mothers, nagging sisters, or girl-friends they were trying to impress?** Discuss to what extent your group members (or other guys they know) need to be "encouraged" or "reminded" by others to work on their spiritual growth. Remind them that maturity is an individual thing. Many of your guys might need to begin to take more responsibility for their own personal growth.

Step 4

Ask each of your guys to think of the detective that best reflects his own personality and style. There are many to choose from: traditional (Sherlock Holmes, Charlie Chan, Nero Wolfe), private eyes (Mike Hammer, Sam Spade, Philip Marlowe, Thomas Magnum, Jim Rockford), police detectives (Columbo, Kojak, Inspector Clouseau, McCloud, Baretta, Ironside), and many more. Monitor your guys' answers for the "cool" factor. Do most of them envision themselves as strong, suave, and smart? After each person has identified with a detective, ask: **If most detectives are guys, why aren't most guys better at solving *spiritual* mysteries?** Let guys respond. Then point out that a better understanding of spiritual matters does not require a "cool factor," but rather a "humility factor." Challenge your guys to be willing to sacrifice the former to acquire the latter.

EXTRA FUN

Step 1

Trivia games seem to be perpetually popular, so open the session with one of your group members' favorites. Try to show how exciting it can be to acquire bits of knowledge about topics that no one *forces* us to learn. Some groups enjoy intellectual stimulation with games such as Trivial Pursuit. Others have favorite syndicated television shows that they can tell you *anything* about (*The Brady Bunch, Gilligan's Island, M*A*S*H*, etc.). Whatever your group members prefer, try to get them involved and enjoying themselves. Then as you go through the session, point out that they should be able to get just as excited about discovering little known facts about various portions of the Bible—including the parts that hardly anyone seems to read.

Step 3

Have a riddle contest to see who can tell the most riddles that stump the rest of the group. You might want to be ready with a few to set the mood. Here are a couple to get you started:

- **Is a dog better dressed in summer or winter?** (In winter he has a coat, but in summer he has a coat and pants.)
- **Who is bigger: Mr. Bigger or Mr. Bigger's son?** (Mr. Bigger's son is a little Bigger.)

If possible, try to find a game called Mindtrap. It contains many challenging word puzzles and riddles that you can use. If you don't have a resource of your own, the kids will probably have plenty of riddles of their own. When you're ready to continue with the session, say: **I have a good one.** Pause. **Oh, but before you tell me the answer, I want you to tell me what the riddle is.** Then introduce the Daniel story.

Step 2
Discuss the classic film *Citizen Kane*. If kids are familiar with it, a discussion should suffice. (Many may have seen it as a classroom assignment.) If not, you might want to have a copy of the videotape cued up in the VCR. If possible, watch the film prior to the meeting to refresh your memory about the plot line. Then, during the meeting, play the tape through the deathbed scene in which Kane speaks the word "Rosebud." Fast-forward through the rest of the movie, narrating over the speeded-up action to let kids know what's happening. Just before the end of the film, as the camera pans through Kane's vast possessions, resume real-time viewing until the secret of Rosebud is revealed and the movie ends. Point out that Kane's last word was an unsolved mystery to those who heard it; yet there was nothing mysterious about it, because *he* knew what he was talking about. Make the same comparison to some of the mysteries of God. We may be completely in the dark as to what some of those things mean, but *God* knows—and that's what matters. Some things we may be able to figure out. Other times we will simply have to trust Him until He chooses to reveal the truth to us.

Step 5
You might want to consider concluding the session with a trip to a local arcade for video games. Or you could set up a few video games in your meeting area. Explain that we don't usually seem to mind mysteries when we're trying to figure out how to save a princess or score enough points to get to the next level. Mysteries can be challenging and fun. The same should be true about spiritual mysteries. We need to devote ourselves to the quest of learning from our mistakes and doing better as we go along—just as we do with a video game. (If you don't have access to enough video games to keep group members occupied and interested, you might consider using the VCR version of the game Clue.)

Step 1
Bring in a "one-minute mystery" book. Such books, which contain short mysteries designed to be solved by asking only yes-or-no questions, can be found in the children's/young adult section of most bookstores. Have kids form two teams. Instruct someone from each team to call out a number at random. (Each number should correspond with a page number in the book.) The number each person calls will determine which mystery you read to his or her team. Have a contest to see which team can solve its mystery using the fewer number of questions. Use this activity to introduce the topic of mysteries in the Bible.

Step 2
Rather than using Repro Resource 9, prepare your own worksheet for your group members. On one side of the sheet, list several symbolic phrases (e.g., "It's raining cats and dogs"; "The early bird gets the worm"; "The grass is always greener on the other side"; etc.). On the other side of the sheet, list the meanings of the phrases. Give your kids one minute to match each phrase with its correct meaning. Award prizes to those who correctly match all of the phrases and meanings within the time limit. Then quickly go through some of the passages listed on Repro Resource 9.

Step 2
Ask your group members to close their eyes and picture the following scenes in their mind. After you set each scene, ask several volunteers to describe how they picture the scene. To set the scenes, read the following:

• *Scene #1*—**See Johnny run. Run, Johnny, run. Run. RUN! I said, Run!**

• *Scene #2*—**Broken glass everywhere . . . Can't take the smell, can't take the noise, got to move out. . . . Rats in the front room, roaches in the back, junkies in the alley with a baseball bat** (Grandmaster Flash and the Furious Five)**.**

• *Scene #3*—**Suddenly the great beast beat its hideous wings, and the wind of them was foul. Again it leaped into the air, and then swiftly fell down upon Eowyn, shrieking, striking with beak and claw** (J.R.R. Tolkien)**.**

Afterward, ask your kids to describe how they picture some of the scenes set by the symbolic language in Revelation.

Step 5
As you wrap up the session, give your kids an opportunity to clear up some of the things they've heard about the end times. Ask volunteers to call out some of the predictions and events they've heard associated with the end times. List group members' responses on the board as they're named. The list might include things like a huge earthquake, a war—probably involving Israel and the Palestinians, the rise of the Antichrist—perhaps from the European Common Market, etc. Point out that certain signs and events may lead some to believe that the end times are just around the corner. But the truth is that we won't know when the last days are coming. Have someone read aloud Matthew 24:36.

COMBINED (Jr. High/High School)

Step 1
Begin the session by handing out paper and pencils only to your junior highers. Ask them: **What do you think are the great mysteries of life? What are some things you think you may never understand?** They may write as many questions as they can think of. When they're finished, collect their papers. Then read the questions at random, asking your high schoolers to answer them. (After all, they are so much older and wiser than the junior highers.) Goad the older kids a bit to make this a matter of pride, so they'll come up with answers that sound logical (whether or not they know what they're talking about). Then point out that certain things remain mysteries for everybody—no matter how old we are—and move on with the session.

Step 4
Because you have some young group members, get a bit more literal as you challenge kids to get more involved with the "remote" portions of the Bible. As kids express what they think are the least meaningful portions of Scripture, use rubber bands and paper clips to show how much of the Bible they are actually talking about. For instance, if someone brings up the Minor Prophets, put a rubber band in your Bible around the books from Hosea to Malachi. When kids are finished naming "non-meaningful" portions of Scripture, use some approximate fractions or percentages to estimate how much of the Bible is left. Ask: **Why do you think God would provide us with a Bible that has _____ pages if all that's important is _____ pages? Why do you think we have so little regard for the parts of the Bible that we've sectioned off?** Point out that we will obviously miss out on a *lot* if we don't expand our Bible study interests. Challenge group members to keep reading the portions of Scripture that are particularly meaningful to them, but also to occasionally explore some of the "unknown" sections of the Bible.

EXTRA CHALLENGE

Step 4
Anticipate some of the answers your group members will give you when you ask about the "least meaningful" portions of Scripture. Be ready with some specific passages in several of the sections of Scripture that sound very confusing at first reading. Let group members struggle with these passages "on the spot." With a little direction from you, they may discover that they can do a pretty good job of figuring out what the passages are saying. Try to give them some spark of encouragement as they begin to recognize that they *can* understand some of the "mysterious" portions of the Bible—if they only try.

Step 5
If group members seem to agree that they should be more adventurous in their approach to the Bible, challenge them to pick a book or passage to study that has always intimidated them. Perhaps one or more of those pesky Minor Prophets needs to be explored. Maybe it's time to try to figure out what Revelation is all about. Encourage kids to decide on something to *try* to study as a group. But be warned: Whatever they decide to study is something you (or someone else) will need to lead. You need to be just as enthusiastic about teaching unfamiliar sections of the Bible as group members are in learning about them.

PLANNING CHECKLIST

Date Used:

Approx. Time

Step 1: It's a Mystery to Me _____
- o Extra Action
- o Small Group
- o Extra Fun
- o Short Meeting Time
- o Combined Jr. High/High School

Step 2: Clanging Symbols _____
- o Large Group
- o Heard It All Before
- o Mostly Girls
- o Media
- o Short Meeting Time
- o Urban

Step 3: In Your Dreams _____
- o Small Group
- o Little Bible Background
- o Fellowship & Worship
- o Mostly Girls
- o Mostly Guys
- o Extra Fun

Step 4: Why Bother? _____
- o Little Bible Background
- o Mostly Guys
- o Combined Jr. High/High School
- o Extra Challenge

Step 5: Hope in the Dark _____
- o Extra Action
- o Large Group
- o Heard It All Before
- o Fellowship & Worship
- o Media
- o Urban
- o Extra Challenge

Custom Curriculum Critique

Please take a moment to fill out this evaluation form, rip it out, fold it, tape it, and send it back to us. This will help us continue to customize products for you. Thanks!

1. Overall, please give this *Custom Curriculum* course (*Your Bible's Alive!*) a grade in terms of how well it worked for you. (A=excellent; B=above average; C=average; D=below average; F=failure) Circle one.

   A B C D F

2. Now assign a grade to each part of this curriculum that you used.

a. Upfront article	A	B	C	D	F	Didn't use
b. Publicity/Clip art	A	B	C	D	F	Didn't use
c. Repro Resource Sheets	A	B	C	D	F	Didn't use
d. Session 1	A	B	C	D	F	Didn't use
e. Session 2	A	B	C	D	F	Didn't use
f. Session 3	A	B	C	D	F	Didn't use
g. Session 4	A	B	C	D	F	Didn't use
h. Session 5	A	B	C	D	F	Didn't use

3. How helpful were the options?
   - ❑ Very helpful
   - ❑ Somewhat helpful
   - ❑ Not too helpful
   - ❑ Not at all helpful

4. Rate the amount of options:
   - ❑ Too many
   - ❑ About the right amount
   - ❑ Too few

5. Tell us how often you used each type of option (4=Always; 3=Sometimes; 2=Seldom; 1=Never)

	4	3	2	1
Extra Action	❑	❑	❑	❑
Combined Jr. High/High School	❑	❑	❑	❑
Urban	❑	❑	❑	❑
Small Group	❑	❑	❑	❑
Large Group	❑	❑	❑	❑
Extra Fun	❑	❑	❑	❑
Heard It All Before	❑	❑	❑	❑
Little Bible Background	❑	❑	❑	❑
Short Meeting Time	❑	❑	❑	❑
Fellowship and Worship	❑	❑	❑	❑
Mostly Guys	❑	❑	❑	❑
Mostly Girls	❑	❑	❑	❑
Media	❑	❑	❑	❑
Extra Challenge (High School only)	❑	❑	❑	❑
Sixth Grade (Jr. High only)	❑	❑	❑	❑

(tape here)

BUSINESS REPLY MAIL
FIRST CLASS MAIL PERMIT NO 1 ELGIN IL

POSTAGE WILL BE PAID BY ADDRESSEE

NO POSTAGE NECESSARY IF MAILED IN THE UNITED STATES

Attn: Youth Department
David C Cook Publishing Co
850 N GROVE AVE
ELGIN IL 60120-9980

6. What did you like best about this course?

7. What suggestions do you have for improving *Custom Curriculum*?

8. Other topics you'd like to see covered in this series:

9. Are you?
   - ❑ Full time paid youthworker
   - ❑ Part time paid youthworker
   - ❑ Volunteer youthworker

10. When did you use *Custom Curriculum*?
   - ❑ Sunday School
   - ❑ Small Group
   - ❑ Youth Group
   - ❑ Retreat
   - ❑ Other ______________________________

11. What grades did you use it with? ______________

12. How many kids used the curriculum in an average week? __________

13. What's the approximate attendance of your entire Sunday school program (Nursery through Adult)? _________

14. If you would like information on other *Custom Curriculum* courses, or other youth products from David C. Cook, please fill out the following:

Name: ______________________________
Church Name: ______________________________
Address: ______________________________
____
Phone: (____) ______________________________

Thank you!